D0942602

NEW BRUNSWICK
BOOK OF
Everything

Everything you wanted to know about
New Brunswick and were going to ask anyway

Martha Walls

MACINTYRE PURCELL PUBLISHING INC.

MacIntyre Purcell Publishing Inc.
First South
Lunenburg, Nova Scotia
B0J 2C0
(902) 482-3152
www.bookofeverything.com

Cover photo courtesy of New Brunswick Department of Tourism and Parks.
Inside Photos. Pages. 8, 30, 38, 60, 92, 108, 135, 180, Courtesy of
New Brunswick Tourism and Parks.
Pages 16,44,164, 123RF. Pages 150, ISTOCKPHOTO

Cover and Design: Channel Communications Inc.

Printed and bound in Canada

Library and Archives Canada Cataloguing in Publication
New Brunswick Book Of Everything : Everything You Wanted To Know About New
Brunswick And Were Going To Ask Anyway / Martha Walls
ISBN 978-0-9738063-2-8
1. New Brunswick--Miscellanea. I. Title..
FC2461.W35 2006   971.5'1   C2006-903321-8

Introduction

No book can truly be about everything, but we hope this gets you close. *The New Brunswick Book of Everything* gives you information about what you should know, about what you'd like to know, and even about what you didn't know you want to know about the 'Picture Province.' From the most delectable New Brunswick ingredients, to the province's most heinous crimes, to its unique slang, it is all here. We tell you about our rich history, how much we earn, what we read, where we work, and even share with you the real deal about the Lake Utopia monster.

We started this project with one guiding principle – to write a book that is interesting, useful, and most importantly, entertaining. We believe that the essence of a place is revealed through the accumulation of detail. You can find it in its physical world of geography and climate, in the pride of its sons and daughters, in local slang, brutal crime and in the quiet park.

We've made it our job to unearth and marshal this detail to reveal a portrait of this fascinating province. We truly could have filled volumes; far too much was lost to editing. To this we say, "next time."

This book was the product of teamwork. Samantha Amara cheerfully tackled a colossal amount of research, writing and editing. Mark Higgins and Mark Taylor contributed their research and writing skills and Alisha Morrissey doggedly tracked down some of our favorite New Brunswickers and their favourite things. We thank those of you who generously offered us Take Fives. You have helped us capture the essence of this unique province and its people. Elva and Judy Purcell poured over the final manuscript searching for inaccuracies and inconsistencies – this is a better book thanks to their efforts. All errors and omissions are our own. We hope that reading this book is as much fun as was putting it together.

New Brunswick lost a long-time resident in 2005. This book is in memory of Beatrice Elliott, a woman who dearly loved her province for all of her 93 years.

Martha Walls, August 2006

Table of Contents

The Land of New Brunswick

In the 1970s, the New Brunswick Department of Tourism sponsored a contest to write a New Brunswick song. The winning entry was by St. Stephen's Donald A. McLeod. His song, "The Land of New Brunswick," has been performed countless times since, each time conjuring up images that are quintessentially New Brunswick.

The Land of New Brunswick

If you want peace of mind leave your worries far behind,
Won't you come back with me to that land down by the sea,
Where the tall timbers grow in the valleys green below,
Reaching up to the hills of New Brunswick.
With the sweet breath of springtime, the smell of new mown hay,
Leaves that turn to red and gold and snow on Christmas Day.
There is kindness to spare, you'll be welcome to a share
of the love and the land of New Brunswick.

La Terre du Nouveau-Brunswick

Si vous voulez la tranquilité l'aissez derrière vos soucis
Revenez avec moi a ce pays près de la mer
Où croissent les grandes épitnettes au bas des vallées vertes
Touchant la cime des collines au Nouveau-Brunswick.
'Vec le vent doux de printemps, et l'arôme du nouveau foin,
Les feuilles qui tournent rouge et or et la neige du jour Noël
On a complaisance pour tous et vous êtes beinvenu à partager
L'amour et la terre au Nouveau-Brunswick. Sis vous wick.

New Brunswick:

A Timeline

1534: Explorer Jacques Cartier names the Bay of Chaleur.

1604: The French establish their first North American colony on St. Croix Island. During the first winter almost half of 79 colonists die of scurvy. In the spring survivors relocate to Port Royal.

1635: Charles de la Tour is granted a huge tract of land in "Nova Scotia," which includes much of New Brunswick.

1654: Nicholas Denys is made Governor of Acadia.

1713: France signs the Treaty of Utrecht, ceding much of French Acadia to England.

1751: Fort Beauséjour is built by the French to challenge British claims to Acadia and to counter the 1749 British construction of Halifax.

1755: The expulsion of the Acadians begins.

1764: Exiled Acadians are allowed to return to New Brunswick. Many return, settling the lower St. John River valley.

1783: 7,000 Loyalists, exiles of the American Revolution, land at Parr Town, present day Saint John.

1784: New Brunswick is separated from Nova Scotia and becomes its own colony.

1785: Saint John is the first Canadian city to be incorporated.

1800: On February 12, the College of New Brunswick, forerunner to Kings College and then the University of New Brunswick, is established.

1812: Black soldiers who fought for Britain during the War of 1812 come to New Brunswick, where they are promised land in exchange for their military service. The promise is broken.

1825: In October, the Great Miramichi Fire burns one-fifth of the province to the ground.

1837: On January 14, fire sweeps through Saint John, wiping out 115 houses and causing $1 million in property damage.

1838: In the heat of August, Saint Johners welcome a new water system that includes fire hydrants to protect the fire-prone city.

1842: The Webster-Ashburton Treaty settles the border dispute between New Brunswick and Maine, but not before troops from both nations amass along the border.

1843: Classes are offered in January at the new Mount Allison Wesleyan Academy, today's Mount Allison University.

1843: On May Day, the province's first official coins, the penny and halfpenny, are minted and circulated.

1850: On November 11, fire destroys much of Fredericton. More than 300 buildings are razed and 2,000 are left homeless.

Bio KLONDIKE KATE KONNECTION

Yes, it's true. Klondike Kate is a New Brunswicker. Born in Johnville in Carleton County, Katherine Ryan was the baby of the family. In 1893, 25-year old Kate found herself living Seattle, yearning to climb western mountains.

In 1897, when prospectors struck gold in the Yukon, she found a reason to head for them thar hills. In 1898 she reached the small tent town of Whitehorse, where she pitched her tent and promptly opened Kate's Café.

By this time the daring young woman was well known, and her business boomed. She expanded her café, eventually moving it to a hotel. She showed her dedication to her adopted town in many ways. She raised funds in support of a Catholic church, acted as community nurse, and offered a laundry service.

The adventuresome young woman earned the nickname Klondike Kate and was known the world over. In later years her good name was sullied when Kitty Rockwell, a prostitute and dancer, assumed Kate's identity, muddying it with public indiscretions and thievery. One might have expected Kate's small hometown to shun the woman vilified in the press, but this was not the case. When Kate returned to Johnville in 1923, she received a hero's welcome. The real Klondike Kate had returned.

1853: North America's first undersea telegraph cable is completed on January 20, connecting Cape Tormentine, NB, and Borden, PEI.

1854: Free trade begins between the United States and Britain, boosting the New Brunswick economy.

1854: New Brunswick gets responsible government.

1859: King's College is renamed the University of New Brunswick.

1867: On July 1, New Brunswick joins Confederation with Ontario, Quebec and Nova Scotia.

1871: A May 17 law establishes free, non-denominational schools, abolishing separate Catholic schools and ruffling a few religious feathers.

1875: Grace Annie Lockhart of Saint John becomes the first woman in the British Empire to earn a university degree when she gets a Bachelor of Science degree from Mount Allison.

1875: In February, two people die in the Caraquet Riot, a dispute over the Common Schools Act.

1877: The largest fire in Saint John's history sets the city ablaze on June 20. It burns for nine hours and leaves more than 13,000 people homeless.

1881: Acadians hold their first Acadian Congress in Memramcook.

1888: The first long-distance phone call is placed between Saint John and Fredericton on July 14.

1889: The University of New Brunswick graduates its first woman, Mary K. Tibbitts of Fredericton, with a Bachelor of Arts (Honours).

1893: The province's first electric trolleys carry passengers through Saint John.

1901: On July 4, the World's Longest Covered Bridge opens in Hartland, offering safe passage over the St. John River.

1910: The town of Campbellton burns to the ground on July 11. When the smoke clears, only four homes are still standing.

1919: New Brunswick women are granted the right to vote provincially.

The Robichaud Revolution

The 1960, election of Liberal Louis J. Robichaud was both a symbolic and a real turning point for the province, especially for Acadian New Brunswick. Acadians, long shut out of power, became cabinet members under Robichaud.

His Equal Opportunity program was designed to raise the fortunes of poor rural regions, many of which were Acadian. He modernized schools in every corner of the province, overhauled the justice system, and implemented standardized public health and welfare programs.

He also set up the University of Moncton, the first Franophone university in the province. Robichaud also made New Brunswick the first and only bilingual province in Canada in 1969. Although Richard Hatfield defeated him in 1970, the Robichaud's decade of political reform endured, prompting future Liberal leader Joseph Daigle to reflect: "He set in granite the pattern for future Liberal policies with his concern for education and opportunity for all regardless of ethnic background or income."

1930: R.B. Bennett, a New Brunswicker from Hopewell, is elected Prime Minister.

1935: On October 15, Willie O'Ree is born in Fredericton; 23 years later he becomes the first black man to play hockey in the NHL.

1950: Fundy National Park, New Brunswick's first National Park, opens to the public in an attempt to protect the area and boost tourism.

1957: The plant that would process the country's first McCain's fries opens, selling 8oz packs for $0.39.

1965: On February 24, New Brunswick's flag flies for the first time.

1969: New Brunswick becomes Canada's only officially bilingual province.

1974: Construction begins at Point Lepreau on the Bay of Fundy, site of the Maritimes' first – and only – nuclear power station.

1987: The Atlantic Canada Opportunities Agency is mandated to create opportunity and employment in Atlantic Canada.

1994: The Congrès Mondial Acadian (Acadian World Congress) is held near Moncton.

1997: After 18 months of construction and with a price tag of $1 billion, the Confederation Bridge opens on June 1, creating a fixed link between New Brunswick and PEI.

2002: Moncton becomes the first officially bilingual city in Canada.

2004: The St.-Anne Nackawic pulp mill in Nackawic unexpectedly closes. 400 people are left jobless, and thousands of others affected. The mill will reopen in 2005, but with a smaller workforce.

2005: In April and May, the St. John River tops its banks, causing the worst flooding in decades.

2005: On September 3, The Rolling Stones rock a crowd of 80,000 near Moncton.

2006: On July 1, gasoline price regulation is adopted by the province.

New Brunswick Essentials

Origin of name: New Brunswick borrowed its name from the duchy of Brunswick in Germany. This duchy was in the possession of Britain's King George III in 1784, the year New Brunswick was established.

License plate: The current plate, in circulation since 1991, features the province's name in French and English and boasts a small galley sailing ship representative of the fishing and shipbuilding industries. There are also other plate options: a conservation license plate features a leaping salmon, firefighters are featured with a plate adorned with their symbol, the Maltese Cross, and a plate featuring a poppy and the words "Veteran-Ancien Combattant" honours veterans. Since 1986 New Brunswickers have had the option personalizing plates with messages of up to seven letters.

Official Name: The Picture Province.

Nick Name: "Herring Choker": Someone who comes from New Brunswick. The term is derived from the stereotype that people living in the Maritimes only eat fish, herring in particular.

Motto: Spem reduxit (*Hope restored*).

Provincial flag: Adopted in 1965, the New Brunswick provincial flag is based on the provincial coat of arms, first designated in 1868. The yellow background is dominated by a galley ship symbolizing the importance of shipbuilding. The ship sails on waves of white and blue. The lion across the top of the flag represents the province's connection with England.

Provincial flower: Purple violet (*Viola cucullata*).

Tartan: Blue, forest green and meadow green, interwoven with gold on red. Adopted in 1959, the New Brunswick tartan was designed by the loomcrofters of Gagetown. Forest green stands for lumbering, meadow green for agriculture, and the blue for coastal and inland waters. These are interwoven with gold, the symbol of New Brunswick's potential wealth. The red blocks symbolize the loyalty of Loyalist settlers and the Royal New Brunswick Regiment.

Provincial bird: Black-capped chickadee (*Poecile atricapillus*). This small songbird features a black cap and bib, white cheeks, buff sides and a distinctive "chickadee-dee-dee" song.

Provincial tree: Balsam fir (*Abies balsamea*). Characterized by its flat, dark green needles and reaching heights of 20 m (65 feet), this adaptable tree is the staple of the provincial pulp and paper and Christmas tree industries.

Did you know...

that New Ireland and Pittsylvania (for British PM William Pitt) were names considered for the new colony of New Brunswick?

Did you know...

that the purple violent is not just an attractive little perennial that graces New Brunswick's fields from May through July? It's also an ingredient in jams and syrups and is used medicinally as a cough suppressant and digestive aid.

Provincial fishing fly: A salmon fly called the "Picture Province" has been New Brunswick's provincial fly since 1993. The fly has a tag of gold symbolizing the value of Atlantic Salmon, a butt of green floss honouring the fiddlehead, and a tail of red goose fibres to match Canada's flag and symbolize New Brunswick's ties with the nation. Its body is cranberry red, one of New Brunswick's official colours, with a rib of gold tinsel. It also has a hackle of lemon yellow (the background colour of the flag), a head of black, and is adorned with a wing of black bear hair.

Time Zone: Atlantic Standard Time.

System of measurement: Metric.

Voting Age: 18

Statutory Holidays: New Year's Day, Good Friday, Canada Day, New Brunswick Day, Labour Day, Remembrance Day and Christmas day. Many employers also recognize Easter Monday, Victoria Day, Thanksgiving Day and Boxing Day.

Capital city: Fredericton.

Did you know...

that New Brunswick has an official provincial soil? Proclaimed in 1997, it is the Holmesville Soil Series. Named for a small town in fertile Carleton County, it is the province's dominant soil type.

City of Stately Elms

Nestled along the banks of the St. John River, the provincial capital of Fredericton has a long and storied history. Well before Europeans came to the area, it was an important Maliseet and Mi'kmaq hunting, fishing and agricultural site. In 1692, a short-lived French fort was erected at the nearby mouth of the Nashwaak River.

The French returned to the area in 1732 when a group of Acadians left peninsular Nova Scotia and established a village at Ste. Anne's Point, the place now occupied by Old Government House. In 1758, Britain, newly in control of all Acadia, razed Ste. Anne's Point and expelled the Acadians. Facing Native resistance, British settlers were slow to settle the area, but by 1768 three British families had settled there.

The year 1783 marked a turning point in the community's history. That October, 2,000 war-weary Loyalist refugees landed at Ste. Anne's Point. Those who survived what was a horrendous first winter fraught with starvation and disease petitioned the government in Halifax to partition Nova Scotia, thereby creating a new province. They got their wish in 1784 when New Brunswick formally came into existence.

In 1785, the town was renamed Frederickstown to honour Prince Frederick, second son of English King George III, although the 'k,' 's' and 'w' were soon dropped. Located 112 km upriver from the mouth of the St. John River, Fredericton was seen as a strategically sound place for the new province's capital, which it was named in April 1785.

The city's inland location presented its own problems. Athough a safe distance from the ocean, the new capital was uncomfortably close to the expansionist-minded United States. With this in mind, Fredericton was fortified with a British military barrack and the presence of Red Coats became a distinguishing feature of the capital.

Did you know...

that King Street in Saint John is the steepest main street in all of Canada?

AMALGAMATION

During the 1990s, the provincial government developed a strategy for municipal restructuring that created large regional governments out of smaller municipalities. The focus was the Miramichi and Saint John areas.

In 1995, the City of Miramichi was formed through an amalgamation of Newcastle, Chatham, Douglastown, Loggieville, Nelson-Miramichi and several surrounding rural communities. In 1998, several communities neighbouring Saint John merged with the city or came together to form the larger towns of Quispamsis, Rothesay and Grand Bay-Westfield.

COUNTIES BY POPULATION

Westmorland	135,103
York	92,306
Gloucester	81,269
Saint John	77,496
Kings	67,990
Northumberland	50,792
Madawaska	35,442

They Said It

"My roots, I'm incredibly proud of them. I believe they are responsible for the success I've had as a negotiator and as a social activist."

— **Buzz Hargrove, president of the Canadian Auto Workers Union and native of Bath, New Brunswick.**

Restigouche	34,889
Kent	31,716
Albert	28,199
Charlotte	28,026
Carleton	27,990
Sunbury	27,339
Victoria	21,298
Queens	12,151

Source: NB Dept of Vital Statistics.

POPULATION IN PERSPECTIVE

New Brunswick is more than five times the size of Connecticut, yet Connecticut has four times as many people. As a percentage of the Canadian population, the population of New Brunswick has been decreasing for more than 60 years as people have left the province to look for better opportunities and as recent immigrants settle in other provinces. Today New Brunswick has just two percent of Canada's population.

BOYS AND GIRLS

Population by age and sex

Age	Males	Females	Total
0-14	62,194	59,323	121,517
15-24	51,853	48,460	100.313
25-44	107,454	106,948	214,402
45-64	104,795	106,268	211,063
65+	44,857	59,854	104,711
Total	371,153	380,853	752,006

Sources: NB Department of Vital Statistics; Statistics Canada

Did you know...

that New Brunswick is Canada's only officially bilingual province?
Source: Government of New Brunswick.

NOT IN THE MILLION CLUB

As of April 1, 2006, 750,504 people called New Brunswick home, down 1,841 from the previous year. The population of New Brunswick is expected to remain stable in 2006. If current birth and out-migration patterns continue, the province is not expected to break the million-people mark any time soon.

Source: NB Dept. of Finance.

Take 5 FIVE FAVOURITE MEMORIES
OF GROWING UP IN NEW BRUNSWICK

David Ganong, president of St. Stephen-based Ganong Bros. Limited, is head of Canada's oldest candy company and a fourth-generation chocolatier. His company is credited with numerous achievements such as inventing the "chicken bone" - sweet cinnamon candy on the outside, semi-sweet dark stuff on the inside – and the chocolate bar. As well, Ganong's products are very popular in Canada and many other countries such as the U.S. and Britain. Through all the success and his travels of the world, Ganong says home remains New Brunswick. He shares with us five things he remembers most about growing up in the province.

1. **Boating with my father in Passmaquoddy Bay** and the islands of Campobello, Deer Island and Passmaquoddy Bay itself.
2. **Tours in the fall of the chocolate factory with my grandfather**, A.D. Ganong, the inventor of the chocolate bar, when the factory was working overtime for Christmas candy.
3. **Trout fishing in the New Brunswick lakes and brooks with my Dad** and friends.
4. **Our family meal out on Sunday night** having hot dogs at the Busy Bee Take-Out, just outside of St. Stephen.
5. **Numerous Scout and Cub camps** at Lake Utopia and weekend camping expeditions with the Scouts.

POPULATION DENSITY

Tokyo	13,416 people/ km^2
New York City	10,194.2 people/km^2
New Brunswick	10.2 people/km^2

Median age
- **Total:** 38.6   women: 39.4   men: 37.7

Life expectancy
- Total: 79.3   women: 82.0   men: 76.5

FERTILITY RATE
- As of 2003, a New Brunswick woman could expect to have 1.4 children in her lifetime.

Sources: NB Department of Vital Statistics; Statistics Canada

ON A TYPICAL DAY IN NEW BRUNSWICK . . .
- 20 children are born
- 18 people die
- 11 marriages take place - three in civil ceremonies and eight by religious clergy
- 4 people divorce

Sources: Statistics Canada and NB Vital Statistics.

Did you know...

that Metepenagiag, a 3,000-year-old Mi'kmaq fishing village, is New Brunswick's oldest continuously occupied community?

Take 5 FIVE MOST POPULOUS
CITIES AND TOWNS

1. **Saint John** — 90,762
2. **Moncton** — 90,359
3. **Fredericton** — 54,068
4. **Miramichi** — 18 508
5. **Bathurst** — 16,427

Source: NB Dept of Vital Statistics.

ORIGIN OF THE SPECIES

Although most New Brunswickers (fully 415,810) were born in Canada, we are a motley crew from a whole host of international and multi-cultural backgrounds.

French	193,470
English	165,235
Irish	135,835
Scottish	127,635
German	27,490
Acadian	26,220
North American Indian	23,815
Dutch (Netherlands)	13,355
Welsh	7,620
Italian	5,610
Métis	4,955

Source: Statistics Canada

Did you know...

that 245,865 New Brunswickers speak both official languages?

MIGRATION TO AND FROM NEW BRUNSWICK

	Out	In
1999-2000	1,183	609
2000-2001	1,530	883
2001-2002	1,218	768
2002-2003	843	648
2003-2004	760	761
2004-2005	1,650	870

Source: NB Department of Finance

IRISH IMMIGRANTS AND RACIAL PREJUDICE

In the late 19th century, Irish immigrants who came to New Brunswick during the Great Famine were quarantined on Partridge Island, near Saint John. Those who survived the journey and escaped quarantine, suffered the wrath of poverty and prejudice in the "Loyalist" city.

The city's Irish population was indispensable in 1877 when Saint John was brought to its knees by the Great Fire. In its aftermath, many townspeople left the city. It was the Irish labourers, who played the biggest part in rebuilding the battered town.

Take 5 TOP FIVE LANGUAGES SPOKEN

1. **English** (65.2 percent)
2. **French** (33.1 percent)
3. **German** (0.2 percent)
4. **Arabic** (0.1 percent)
5. **Mi'kmaq** (less than 0.1 percent)

Source: Statistics Canada.

THE MARRYING KIND

The average age of first marriage in New Brunswick is 27.3 for brides and 29.6 years for grooms. Compare that to 25 years ago, when the ages were 24.8 years for women and 27.3 years for men. In 2005 there were 3,846 marriages in New Brunswick.

Source: Statistics Canada

FAMILY STRUCTURE

- Percentage of children living in married two-parent households: 69
- Common law, two-parent families: 9.3
- Female lone-parent families: 18
- Male lone-parent families: 3.8

Source: Statistics Canada

D-I-V-O-R-C-E

- Divorce rate (per 100,000) in New Brunswick: 37.6
- Divorce rate in Canada: 48.8
- In 2003 there were 1,450 divorces in New Brunswick.

Source: Statistics Canada,

RELIGIOUS AFFILIATION

- Roman Catholic: 53.6 percent
- Protestant: 36.5 percent
- Muslim: 0.2 percent
- Jewish: 0.1 percent
- Hindu: 0.1 percent
- Buddhist: 0.1 percent
- No religious affiliation: 8 percent

Source: Statistics Canada.

HEALTH CARE PROFESSIONALS
(2006 FIGURES UNLESS OTHERWISE INDICATED)

Physicians	1,370
Dentists	285
Registered Nurses (2005)	8,458
Licensed Practical Nurses (2005)	3,065
Physiotherapists	455
Pharmacists	625

Sources: NB Department of Health, NB Dental Society, Nurses Association of New Brunswick, Association of New Brunswick Licensed Practical Nurses, NB College of Physiotherapists, NB Pharmacists' Association.

EDUCATIONAL INSTITUTIONS

Universities	4 public, 3 private
Colleges, NB Community College,	11 campuses
English schools, P-12 (03/04)	236
Francophone schools, P-12 (03/04)	102

Source: Government of New Brunswick.

FULL-TIME ENROLLMENT

Universities, 2004-2005	24,808
NBCC, 2004-2005	18,867
Other colleges, 2005-2006	3,077
Public Schools, P-12, 2004-2006	114,820
Private schools, P-12	1,000

Sources: Maritime Provinces Higher Education Commission; NB Dept. of Post-Secondary Education; NB Dept of Education.

COMMUNICATIONS (2006)

Daily/weekly newspapers	30
TV/cable broadcasting source stations	7
AM / FM radio stations	44

Source: Communications New Brunswick.

INTERNET

As of 2003, 53.3 percent of New Brunswick households used the Internet from some location: 42.7 percent use it from home, 28.9 percent from work, and 18.2 percent from school. Wireless Internet also has a foothold in the province, with 34 Wi-Fi locations across the province according to Jwire (a website that tracks wireless hotspots around the globe). Most of these are in Fredericton. Since 2003 the capital city has been committed to creating a wireless Internet zone, dubbed the Fred e-zone.

Source: Statistics Canada.

Weblinks

Miscellaneous New Brunswick

www.new-brunswick.net

This New Brunswick website is filled with an entertaining array of facts, stories and other information about the picture province.

Newspapers

www.canadaeast.com

Want to catch up on the news in New Brunswick? Check out this website featuring the main newspapers of New Brunswick published by Brunswick News.

Place names

When it comes to place names, New Brunswickers owe a huge debt to the province's first people. Many places bear Mi'kmaq, Maliseet and Passamaquoddy names and serve as a lasting testament to their intimate knowledge of the land. Europeans also left their marks on the map with their references to their homelands and politicians who, for some reason, they wished to immortalize cartographically.

Alma (Albert County): Known as the quaint little town entrance of Fundy National Park, this seaside community gets its name from the 1855 Crimean War battle of Alma River fought the year before Alma was founded.

Apohaqui (Kings County): This birthplace of Frank McKenna may get its name from a Maliseet word meaning "junction of two streams"; the community is near the juncture of the Millstream and Clements brooks.

Baie Ste. Anne (Northumberland County): Located on Miramichi Bay, this community was first settled by anxious Acadians in 1760 who, just five years after deportation, returned unlawfully to Acadia. It is named for Ste. Anne, mother of the Virgin Mary, and also the spiritual guardian of Catholic Mi'kmaw.

Bathurst (Gloucester County): First known in 1852 as Nepisiguit, and later as St. Peters, Bathurst got its current handle in 1826. The Governor of Nova Scotia named it for a British politician, Henry, third Earl of Bathurst.

Belledune (Gloucester County): Home to the "beautiful dunes" that give it its name, Belledune is located on a deep harbour of the Bay of Chaleur. It has become known somewhat infamously as the home of one of the world's largest lead and zinc smelters, which are alleged to have contaminated the area.

Big Bald Mountain (Northumberland County): Raising 762 m, this topographical feature is, well, a big bald mountain.

Boiestown (Northumberland County): A testament to the province's forest industry, was named after American Thomas Boies. By the 1930s he had established this company town to house his sawmill employees.

Chance Harbour (Saint John County): First settled by Loyalists in 1784, its name refers to the navigational hazards associated with the harbour's mouth.

Dieppe (Westmorland County): Known for many years as Leger Corner, the community was renamed in 1946 in honour of Canadian soldiers who fell at the World War Two Battle of Dieppe, August 19, 1942.

Doaktown (Northumberland County): This town on the mighty Miramichi was without a name until the 1850s. Only when a post office was established there in 1853 did the name of settler Robert Doak rescue the town from a nameless fate.

Edmundston (Madawaska County): This city occupies the junction of the St. John and Madawaska Rivers. Known originally as Petit-Sault or 'little falls', the name was changed in 1850 to honour New Brunswick Lieutenant Governor, Sir Edmund Bond Head.

Saint John

Situated at the mouth of the St. John River, Saint John is New Brunswick's largest city. The river was named by Samuel de Champlain, who sailed into the river's harbour in 1604 for the feast of St. John the Baptist. In 1630, Charles de la Tour, Lieutenant Governor of Acadia from 1631 to 1635, built the first permanent settlement at the site of present-day Saint John, which he modestly named Fort La Tour.

By 1758 the fort had been taken and occupied by the English, who renamed it Fort Fredrick. Seventeen years later, American revolutionaries destroyed Fort Frederick, replacing it as Fort Howe. Following the American Revolution, the founders of Fort Howe returned to their new nation and were replaced by the refugee United Empire Loyalists, who founded the nearby settlements of Parr Town and Carleton. In 1785, Parr Town and Carleton amalgamated as Canada's first incorporated city—Saint John.

Saint John served briefly as the provincial capital, but that title was soon handed over to Fredericton. With its political aspirations cut short, Saint John began to concentrate on economic growth. Situated at the mouth of the St. John River, perfect for transporting logs, a booming timber trade sprang up and earned Saint John one of the largest fleets of wooden sailing ships in the entire British Empire. The city became famous for the *Marco Polo*, a schooner built in the port city that was known as "the fastest ship in the world."

Florenceville (Carleton County): Nestled along the St. John River, this one-time "Buttermilk Creek" was renamed Florenceville in 1855, during the Crimean War. It was named to commemorate the unfailing devotion of war nurse, Florence Nightingale.

Fort Folly Point (Westmorland County): This area juts into Shepody Bay, at the mouth of the Memramcook and Petitcodiac Rivers. Some think it was the site of Jonathan Eddy's failed rebellion during the American Rev. O the treacherous waters offshore.

Grand Falls/Grand-Sault (Victoria County): This is a bit of a no-brainer. This town is named for the 23 m falls that occur at this site on the St. John River. This is the only New Brunswick community to officially have a bilingual name.

Hartland (Carleton County): Famously home to the world's longest covered bridge, this town gets its name from James Hartley, a surveyor and MLA for the county in which it is found. Hartland is the birth-place of the late Premier Richard Hatfield.

Hillsborough (Albert County): This township near Moncton was created in 1765, named for Wills Hill, Earl of Hillsborough. For a time after the 1766 settlement of Germans from Pennsylvania the name Dutch Village replaced Hillsborough, but the original name stood the test of time.

Jemseg (Queens County): Located at the southern tip of Grand Lake, Jemseg is a corrupted version of the Maliseet 'ah-jim-sek', meaning 'pick up place'. The Maliseet long used this place to cache supplies.

Perth-Andover (Victoria County): Founded in 1833 as the Parish of Andover (which was borrowed from England and means 'ash tree stream'), the community of Andover and Perth, named for a Scottish city, combined forces in 1966.

Point Lepreau (Charlotte County): Today the home of the nuclear generating station that bears this name, its name probably is a corruption of the French "la pereau," meaning "little rabbit."

Renforth (Kings County): Located on Kennebecassis Bay, this community was named for James Renforth, a member of a boat crew from Newcastle-upon-Tyne, England, who died while racing a crew from Saint John in an 1871 regatta.

Rexton (Kent County): First named Kingston after a place in England, the town pragmatically changed its name in 1901 so as to avoid confusion with the many other Kingstons on the New Brunswick map.

Roachville (Kings County): This place name has a far more pleasant origin than you might think; Loyalist John Roach was the area's first settler.

St. Andrews (Charlotte County): This lovely tourist town at the mouth of the St. Croix river got its start long before the Loyalists inundated the area. As the story goes, a French missionary landed at the spot on St. Andrew's Day (November 30) and named the site after the revered saint. In 1783, Loyalists settled down the coast at present day Castine, Maine; however, when the St. Croix was named the international boundary between New Brunswick and the USA, they disassembled their homes and moved them to St. Andrews, on the British side of that boundary. In the 1880s, the seaside community found its tourist groove and became known as a seaside mecca, Saint-Andrews-by-the-Sea

Saint-Antoine (Kent County): Established around the year 1700, it was named after a Récollet missionary. It is also the birthplace of Premier Louis J. Robichaud.

Saint-Quentin (Restigouche County): Originally known as 'Five Fingers' after a local brook and renamed Anderson Sidining in 1910, this town got its modern name relatively late. It was named in 1919 for a battle won by the allies during WWI.

Seven Days Work (Charlotte County): This cliff face on Grand Manan Island boasts seven identifiable layers of rock. The name also references the Genesis creation story.

Skeedaddle Ridge (Carleton County): During the American Civil War, this spot was said to be a haven for draft-dodgers who fled their tours of duty with the Northern Army by 'skeedaddling' here.

The Wolves (Charlotte County): These three islands in Passamaquoddy Bay — Eastern Wolf, Flat Wolf and Southern Wolf — have since 1707 been associated with wolves. According to Native lore, Glooscap was once watching three wolves chasing a deer and moose. When he noticed the hunted growing weary, he turned all the creatures into islands. Moose Island, Maine and Deer Island, NB are nearby.

Woodstock (Carelton County): So named since its founding in 1786, Woodstock harkens back to a town of the same name in England. The name meant 'a place in the woods,' appropriate enough for this little town nestled at the confluence of the Meduxnekeag and St. John Rivers. Woodstock was incorporated in 1856, the first among New Brunswick's current towns to do so.

Zealand (York County): Founded by British settlers in 1867, the year of Confederation, it was first known as New Zealand, after the country. In 1961, the town was old enough to become just plain Zealand.

New Brunswick Slang:

Every region of the world has its own distinct language. Words and expressions, nurtured and given meaning over time, inform the jokes we tell and provide those of us living here with a collective shorthand that identifies us as New Brunswickers. New Brunswick is blessed with a rich language that varies from county to county, and city to city. Here's a small sampling.

Across the lines: Across the international border into the United States

Alma sticky buns: This isn't what you think. These delectable cinnamon buns are sold at Kelly's Bake Shop in the seaside town of Alma.

Black flies: Okay, okay, so these pests are not unique to New Brunswick. But we feel you can't really know the meaning of this word until you've spent time outdoors in New Brunswick in the spring.

Blat: To cry or whine.

Bogtrotter: A term for a resident of New Brunswick. Also a pejorative term for an Irish person. New Brunswick's preponderance of people of Irish descent probably explains its connection to the province.

Bootiner: In a rush or hurrying.

Take 5 JOHN MORRIS' TOP FIVE
CARLETON COUNTY WORDS

John Morris, Editor in Chief, of Carleton County Colloquialisms (CCC) was born and bred in Carleton County. He created the CCC website in a fit of homesickness while living in the US. Morris has returned to his Carelton County "homeland"; he and is wife now live in Woodstock, NB.

1. **jumpins** Also: holy jumpins; An exclamation of surprise, fascination, or frustration; "Oh, jumpins! You scared the heck outta me!" Occasionally "jumpins" is used as a sentence all on its own. Origin unknown, although usage and etymology suggests a link to the pejorative usage of "Jesus" and similar sounding words, or perhaps an alternate form of "liftin'". Usage appears to be limited to western and central Carleton County.

2. **holy-liftin'** An exclamation of surprise, fascination, or frustration; "Holy-liftin'! These mittens cost $20!" Origin unknown, but etymology suggests a reference to the resurrection of Christ ("Holy-liftin' Lordy" is a common derivative). This is consistent with the regional practice of cussing through iconoclastic reference: similar terms are used in local French dialects. The theological associations of such terms, however, have been largely forgotten in English-speaking communities. Holy-liftin' is quite versatile, and may be truncated ("liftin'") conflated ("holy-ol'-liftin'") or pluralized ("liftin's") at the speaker's whim. The ressurection imagery is reinforced by another popular usage, "holy-liftin' dyin'," or sometimes just "holy dyin'." Both "liftin'" and "dyin'" are frequently employed in the regional habit of elaborate compound-cussing, e.g.: "Holy ol' liftin' dyin' bald-headed Jesus!"

3. **piss-cut** Most often used in the gerundive form "piss-cuttin'". The term denotes excessive speed, associated with recklessness or an out-of-control situation; "We was doin' at least 90; just piss-cuttin' 'er!"

4. **float** Go away, depart, scat; used always in the imperative; "Git! G'wan! Float, ya little christer!" Commonly used to repel cats, small dogs, and children.

5. **spleeny** To be incapable of enduring physical pain; "Rhonda skun her knee and she cried all day - she's some spleeny, that girl."

Boughten bread: Bread purchased at a store, as opposed to home-made bread. Usually sliced.

Buddy: A generic name for "that fellah," or any person whose name one does not know.

Chimley: Phonetically, a New Brunswicker's pronunciation of the word "chimney."

Cuff: To strike, usually another person. Also to skip class at school.

Dooryard: The front lawn.

Downriver: To travel south along the Saint John River.

Dulse: Dried salted seaweed, eaten as a snack.

'English Muffin': A slightly pejorative Francophone nickname for an Anglophone New Brunswicker.

Fiddlehead: A seasonal green, the young shoots of ferns, harvested in spring. They can be eaten steamed, boiled or as part of pastas and stir-frys, though some say they are best smothered in butter or vinegar.

Fiddleheading: The onerous black-fly plagued process of picking fiddleheads, which grow in swamp ground along freshwater rivers.

Frederictonians: The residents of Fredericton, the capital city.

Frenglish: A blend of English and French spoken in bilingual New Brunswick.

"Holy liftin'!": An exclamation of shock or surprise.

Hub City: The city of Moncton.

Imagine: Who would have thought?

King Cole: New Brunswick-made black tea. To many New Brunswickers, the only beverage worthy of teatime.

KV: The Kennebecasis valley.

Irving, The: The local gas station, most of which in New Brunswick are owned by Irving Oil Limited, founded by New Brunswick entrepreneur and oil magnate, the late KC Irving.

Lad: A young boy, or a male friend. Use is especially common in Miramichi.

L.C., The: The Liquor Commission, the provincial sellers of all beer, wine and spirits in New Brunswick.

Lunch bucket: The container in which you carry your lunch to work or school.

Monctonians: People from Moncton.

Moosehead: A beer manufactured in Saint John, New Brunswick at Canada's oldest independent brewery.

Overhome: Your house; the place you grew up and to which you return with some frequency.

Peeling tires: The practice of squealing ones tires, which, for males, can be a means of demonstrating manliness.

Potato break: A two week vacation from school granted to children living in the potato belt of New Brunswick in September so they could participate in the fall potato harvest.

Rappie pie: An Acadian delicacy featuring chicken and/or pork and potatoes, combined in a casserole. It is sometimes served with molasses.

Renous: A community near Miramichi, but for most New Brunswickers, it's the federal maximum-security penitentiary located nearby.

Right out of'er: To be incapacitated, usually drunk.

Saint Johners: People from Saint John.

So didn't I: Me too; so did I.

Spleeny: Wimpy and unable to tolerate pain or any adverse conditions.

Sweets: Frederictonians, especially those under age 21, will instantly recognize this as the nickname of Sweetwaters dance bar in downtown Fredericton.

Tourtiere: An Acadian meat pie, usually featuring pork but also mixed with veal or rabbit.

The Sugar: Diabetes, denoted as "having a touch of the sugar."

Timmies: Tim Hortons, the ubiquitous Canadian coffee chain with 121 stores in the province.

Two-four: A case of 24 beer.

Upriver: To travel north, up the Saint John River.

Uptown: What Saint Johners, confusingly enough, call their down-town area.

Warsh: A New Brunswicker's rendition of the word "wash".

White poultice: A late-spring snowstorm, so called for the positive effect it was said to have on crops.

Very best: A reply to "How are you?", meaning "I'm fine, thank you."

Yas/youse: You guys.

Weblinks

Carleton County Colloquialisms
http://www.dooryard.ca/indexIntro.html
This hilarious and interactive website offers the A-Z of the words and phrases that distinguish those from Carleton County, New Brunswick, from all other people on the globe.

Natural World

Covering nearly 73,000 km², the province of New Brunswick contains less than one percent of Canada's total landmass. It is the third smallest Canadian province, ahead only of Nova Scotia and Prince Edward Island. Although small by Canadian standards, New Brunswick is no slouch on the international stage; it is as big as Panama, nearly double the size of both Denmark and the Netherlands, and is more than six times larger than Jamaica. As a U.S. state, the province would be wedged in between South Carolina and West Virginia, which rank 40th and 41st in size.

LONGITUDE AND LATITUDE
On the global grid, Fredericton is located at 45°57' N latitude and 66°40' W longitude. This places it on near-par latitude with capitals like Ottawa, Sofia, Bulgaria and Vienna, Austria, and along the same longitude lines as La Paz, Bolivia, San Juan, Puerto Rico and Caracas, Venezuela.

PHYSICAL SETTING
- Area   73,440 km²
- Length   322 km (north to south)

- Average width   242 km (east to west)
- Furthest distance to the ocean   180 km
- Mainland coastline   1,850 km

SEEING THE TREES FOR THE FOREST

When the first European settlers came to New Brunswick, they were in awe of the dense mixed forests. The province is still covered in trees. For its size, the province has more trees than any other part of the country and is one of the most forested areas in the world. About 85 percent of the province is forested, amounting to 6.1 million hectares

Take 5 — FIVE MOST COMMON TREE SPECIES

1. **Spruce** (31 percent)
2. **Balsam Fir** (19 percent)
3. **Sugar Maple, Red Maple** (8 percent each)
4. **Cedar, Poplar** (7 percent each)
5. **White Birch, Yellow Birch** (5 percent each)

Source: Government of New Brunswick.

Take 5 — TOP FIVE PEAKS

1. **Mount Carleton** (817 m)
2. **Mount Edward** (800 m)
3. **Mount Head** (800 m)
4. **Nalaisk Mountain** (785 m)
5. **Sagamook Mountain** (785 m)

Source: Natural Resources Canada.

of forest. Roughly 50 percent is Crown land.

- Percentage of forest lands that is softwood: 46 percent
- Percentage of forest lands that is hardwood: 27 percent
- Percentage of forest lands that is mixed wood: 27 percent

Sources: Natural Resources Canada; Government of New Brunswick.

MOTHER NATURE'S PRUNING

Between 350 and 400 fires sweep across New Brunswick, devastating nearly 550 hectares of forest every summer. In recent years, however, incidences of fire have fallen off. In 2004 there were only 254 fires, which ravaged 288 hectares. The most destructive forest fire season in recent years was 1986 when 588 wildfires reduced nearly 40,000 hectares of forest to ash.

Source: Government of New Brunswick.

THE AUTUMN NEW BRUNSWICK BURNED

The summer and fall of 1825 were extremely hot and dry in central New Brunswick. On the afternoon of October 7, 1825 a huge column of smoke was spied rising out of the woods; by evening an inferno, the largest in the history of northeastern North America, was raging in the woods near Miramichi.

An estimated 15 550 km², a huge triangle of woodland stretching

Did you know...

that the Christmas Mountains were once slated to be named after Santa's Reindeer, with Rudolph Mountain being the highest peak? So named for the range's proximity to the North Pole Stream, this idea was deemed too commercial and this peak was renamed St. Nicholas Mountain. The name Christmas Mountains, though not official, is widely used. The area is home to the province's largest stand of virgin forest.

from Fredericton to Richibucto to Belledune, went up in smoke that day. An astonishing 20 percent of the province burned to the ground. The village of Newcastle was reduced to embers. Thousands were left homeless and as many as 300 people died in the flames or by drowning as they fled the wall of fire.

A number of possible causes for the blaze have been put forward. One is that the bark and branches left by lumbermen as they felled and squared trees in the woods had somehow sparked the blaze. Another explanation is that lightening is to blame.

WATER, WATER EVERYWHERE

Like the other Atlantic Provinces, the waters in and around New Brunswick have played a major role in its history and development. No part of the province is more than 180 km away from the ocean and the vast number of lakes, rivers and tributaries throughout the province have helped shape its economy and culture.

Did you know...

that in 2005 a student at Mount Allison university discovered the world's oldest Red Spruce, right here in New Brunswick? Judging from the rings of its trunk, scientists believe it to be 445 years old.

They Said It

"The tree itself just has this glow about it. You can tell it's significant when you approach it."

— Ben Phillips to the CBC, on his discovery
of the globe's oldest Red Spruce.

They Said It

"A loud roaring was heard in the woods . . . [and] . . . it was so dark that the flames could not be distinguished though they were more than one mile from the town. Immediately after, the wind blew a hurricane, a roaring noise became more and more tremendous and seemed to the astonished people as if the earth had loosened from its ancient foundation."

— An eyewitness to the great fire of 1825

ISLANDS

New Brunswick's three coastlines are home to no fewer than nine coastal islands which attract tourists and locals alike. They are known for their beauty and, in some cases, for their famous inhabitants.

- Campobello Island: The site of former U.S. President Franklin D. Roosevelt's summer home.
- Deer Island: Home to the western hemisphere's largest tidal pool.
- Grand Manan Island: Fertile offshores make this the dulse capital of the world.
- Miscou Island: Known for its white sandy beaches and fiery red peat bogs.

Take 5 FIVE MOST IMPORTANT CROPS IN NEW BRUNSWICK

1. **Potatoes**
2. **Grass** (in the form of hay and pasture)
3. **Greenhouse and nursery**
4. **Grain**
5. **Blueberries**

Source: New Brunswick Department of Agriculture, Fisheries and Aquaculture.

- Lameque Island: Sister isle to Miscou, this spot also boasts red peat.
- Jourimain Island: This bird sanctuary offers splendid bird watching.
- Irving Nature Park Island: Boasts 12 km of trails along the Bay of Fundy.
- Ministers Island: At low tide you can drive your car along the ocean floor and visit the haven owned by Canadian Pacific Railway builder, Sir William Van Horne.
- Head Harbour Island: Accessible by foot – and only during low tide – this is home to New Brunswick's oldest lighthouse.

Source: Tourism New Brunswick.

Take 5 — BYRON 'BYZIE' COUGHLAN'S FIVE FAVORITE RIVERS TO FLY FISH FOR SALMON

Byron 'Byzie' Coughlan is the owner and operator of Miramichi Country Haven Lodge and Cottages located in Grey Rapids on the Main Southwest Miramichi River. "Nothing is more enjoyable than to fish these waters as a child into adulthood. I get to teach the art of fly fishing for Atlantic Salmon to young and old from around the world and see the joy on people's faces when the greatest game fish of them all breaks the surface. This is not work, this is my life, a great life!"

1. The Main **Southwest Miramichi** is approximately 220 miles, running from Juniper and emptying into the St. Lawrence Seaway. It is considered the most productive river of the Miramichi system. The Miramichi River running through central New Brunswick produces over half of the Atlantic salmon of the world and empties into a number of tributaries that support the sport of fly fishing to sportsmen from all over the world. Both public and private waters allow novice and experts to try their hand at catching the King of Fish — the Atlantic salmon.

BEACHES

Most of the Atlantic region is known for its icy waters, sometimes even in the middle of July. But it is a little known fact that some of the warmest saltwater beaches north of Virginia can be enjoyed in New Brunswick. Included on this list is the popular Parlee Beach as well as Kelly's Beach in Kouchibouguac National Park, where waters can hit 30°C.

- Number of publicly accessible beaches in New Brunswick: 40 saltwater and 20 freshwater

Source: Tourism New Brunswick.

2. The **Northwest Miramichi River** is the earliest producing tributary of the Miramichi system and is considered the most productive tributary.

3. The **Renous River** is one of the smaller tributaries but excellent for early summer and fall Atlantic salmon fishing. It is nestled amongst some of nature's greatest scenery.

4. The **Cain's River** is a scenic little river renowned for its fall salmon runs. It goes through northeastern New Brunswick hinterlands meeting the Miramichi some twenty miles above the Tidal water. This tributary is extremely enjoyable to canoe and fish, especially during the autumn foliage.

5. The **Restigouche River** located in northern New Brunswick forms the provincial boundary between New Brunswick and Quebec. At 152 km long, it goes through deep forest and hills and is not as big a producer of Atlantic salmon as the Miramichi, although it has always been famous for its run of larger salmon.

Take 5 FIVE LARGEST
COASTAL ISLANDS IN NEW BRUNSWICK

1. **Lameque Island** – 150 km^2
2. **Grand Manan Island** – 137 km^2
3. **Campobello Island** – 70 km^2
4. **Miscou Island** – 64 km^2
5. **Deer Island** – 45 km^2

Source: Tourism New Brunswick.

WATER

- Percentage of the total landmass of New Brunswick that is fresh water: 2
- Number of major rivers: 27

Source: Source: Natural Resources Canada.

GO JUMP IN THE (GRAND) LAKE

The largest lake in New Brunswick is Grand Lake, located 40 km east of Fredericton and 28 km away from the Bay of Fundy. No small pond, the lake covers 173.5 km^2 – compare that to the 131.2 km^2 the city of

Take 5 THE FIVE LONGEST
RIVERS IN NEW BRUNSWICK

1. **St. John River:** 673 km
2. **Miramichi River:** 250 km
3. **Aroostook River:** 225 km
4. **Restigouche River:** 200 km
5. **Magaguadavic River and Petitcodiac River:** 129 km (tie)

Source: Natural Resources Canada.

Take 5 THE TOP FIVE
NATURAL RESOURCES

1. **Forest**
2. **Mineral Deposits**
3. **Agriculture**
4. **Fisheries**
5. **Fish and Game** (as recreation)

Source: Canadian Encyclopedia.

Fredericton covers – and measures 32 km by 11.2 km. Only about 2 m above sea level and reaching a depth of 30.5 m, Grand Lake offers up waves of over 2 m in a storm and nourishes the soil all around it. In fact, 50 percent of the province's fresh produce comes from the Grand Lake area.

Source: Grand Lake informational website.

RHINE OF NORTH AMERICA

The Saint John River rises in northwestern Maine, meandering through the state and forming part of the U.S.-Canada border. Near Grand Falls the river switches course and flows though New Brunswick, heading south through the Upper St. John River Valley, flows southeast, passing through Fredericton – where it is nicknamed the 'Rhine of North America' – before ending its 673-km journey and emptying into the Bay of Fundy at Saint John.

It is here that riverwatchers can marvel at a unique natural phenomenon. Twice a day, the waters rushing in for high tide in the Bay

Did you know...

that the more than 100 billion tonnes of saltwater that flow in and out of the Bay of Fundy is more than the flow of all the world's freshwater rivers combined?

of Fundy – highest tides in the world – force the waters of the mighty St. John River to flow backwards, creating the Reversing Falls Rapids, one of the province's prime tourist attractions.

The St. John River, which at Clair, New Brunswick, flows at a rate of up to 151,000 cubic feet per second, has been integral in the history and development of the province. Everyone from the First Nations and Sameul de Champlain to the Acadians and early European settlers have benefitted from this tremendous waterway. Throughout its history, the river has provided a travel and trade route, a cargo channel on which logs float to saw mills in the south and, more recently, an invaluable source of hydroelectric power.

BAY OF FUNDY

There has long been some debate as to whether the world's highest tides occur in the Bay of Fundy or in Quebec's Ungava Bay. However, the Canadian Hydrographic Service (CHS) has finally weighed in and declared it a 'statistical' tie. (CHS says tides In Ungava Bay have been measured up to 16.8 m while those in the Bay of Fundy have reached 17 m.)

Bay of Fundy supporters, however, have been able to parlay that additional 0.2 m into something much greater. The Bay is known around the globe as home to the highest tides in the world and each

Did you know...

that the most northern point in New Brunswick is the Inch Arran Lighthouse, not far from Dalhousie?

Did you know...

that Chaleur Beach in Restigouche County is home to one of the world's longest natural sand bars? The Eel River Bar stretches 1.5 km and gives swimmers the best of both worlds. Salt water of Chaleur Bay on one side and the Eel River freshwater on the other.

year draws waves of tourists. The Bay's coastline stretches over 1,700 km between New Brunswick and Nova Scotia and is washed afresh each day by about 100 billion tonnes of seawater. The history of the Bay stretches back with time itself – the Mi'kmaq explain that a giant splashing whale caused the tides.

HERE KITTY, KITTY

Does too! Does not! Perhaps no wildlife issue is more hotly debated than the question of whether the eastern cougar still roams the woods of New Brunswick. The last confirmed sighting of this large tawny cat

Take 5 FIVE "MUST SEE"
NATURAL TOURIST ATTRACTIONS

1. **Cape Enrage**, named by Frommer's Guide as the best view in Canada, for its panoramic view of the bay of Fundy.

2. **Cape Jourimain Nature Centre**, a community-run ecotourism and environmental education facility on the Northumberland Straight, on the New Brunswick side of the Confederation Bridge.

3. **Kingsbrae Garden** in St. Andrews has over 50,000 flowering plants, shrubs. An enchanting horticultural masterpiece, Kingsbrae Garden is balm for the soul.

4. **Grand Falls Gorge**, an impressive waterfall, 70 m high in parts, in the heart of downtown Grand Falls.

5. **Irving Nature Park**, allows you to experience the topography and animal life of coastal southern New Brunswick on the outskirts of Saint John.

Source: New Brunswick Department of Tourism.

They Said It

was recorded almost 75 years ago, when a hunter shot one of the mammoth felines. But this fact hasn't stopped speculation that the wild cat still roams the province's dense forests.

It seems even the identity of this critter is now up for debate. It was

Take 5 MIKE MEADE'S FIVE FAVOURITE
PLACES TO ROCK CLIMB IN NEW BRUNSWICK

Mike Meade is an avid photographer and rock climber. His two passions frequently take him to some of New Brunswick's most picturesque and lofty locations. These are some of his favourite places in New Brunswick to scale rock walls – and to take photos from an eagle's eye view.

1. Cochrane Lane Cliffs, Welsford: Located off Route 7 between Fredericton and Saint John, this area boasts excellent sport and traditional climbing on granite, with over 300 documented routes and many scenic vistas. Since the cliffs are on CFB Gagetown property, the general public must procure a day pass for "Area 40" at Camp Petersville. For more information on access, call CFB Gagetown at 1-506-422-2000. Information on obtaining a guidebook is available at www.climbeasterncanada.com.

2. Greenlaw, St. Andrews: This is a relatively new climbing area located off Route 127 from Fredericton. The variety of features in the basalt rock combined with more than 20 established sport

Did you know...

that provincial legislation protects 16 animal and plant species in New Brunswick?

once believed that the cat was part of an eastern subspecies of cougar, but biologists now think that the New Brunswick cat, if it exists, is part of same cougar family that inhabits western Canada.

Since the 1970s, many New Brunswickers from all regions have claimed to have seen an eastern cougar. Each year 40 sightings are

routes, some nearby boulder problems, and its proximity to picturesque St. Andrews make this a captivating little climbing craig.

3. Bald Peak, Welsford: Just off Route 101 in Welsford, this small and enticing granite cliff features an extended bare-rock peak and a good variety of shorter climbing routes. Bald Peak is a great spot for those new to the sport of climbing or for those looking for a good warm-up craig.

4. UNB Woodlot, Fredericton: The numerous boulder problems on the banks of a peaceful bubbling brook make the UNB woodlot a popular destination for many of the capital city's climbers. There are also a few short caves that make for some challenging climbs.

5. UNB Climbing Wall, Fredericton: This indoor facility, run by the UNB Rock and Ice Climbing Club, is perfect for the height-shy beginner as well as the training enthusiast. It is generally open weekday evenings, and can be booked for children's birthday parties on weekends during the fall and winter months. For more information, E-mail the club president at climb@unb.ca.

Take 5 — FIVE PROTECTED ANIMALS

1. Leatherback turtle
2. Eastern cougar
3. Harlequin duck
4. Maritime Ringlette butterfly
5. Peregrine falcon

reported. The problem is, no one can prove it. At up to 9 feet long, 30 inches high, and 150 lbs, there is no chance you would confuse one of these animals with Ginger, your cat. The Department of Natural Resources investigates all credible sightings, and these have resulted in tantalizing circumstantial evidence.

In 1992 biologists found tracks belonging to a very large pussycat near Juniper. Hair found in scat deposited near these tracks was also confirmed to belong to a cougar. Until more evidence is gathered, however, feline fiends will have to speculate about the existence of the Felis concolor cougar. But take heart! No one, it seems, is willing to say for sure that the creature doesn't exist; the province considers it an endangered species and offers it full protection.

Take 5 — FIVE PROTECTED PLANTS

1. Anticosti aster
2. Bathurst aster
3. Furbish's lousewort
4. Gulf of St. Lawrence aster
5. Parker's pipewort

Source: New Brunswick Federation of Naturalists.

Weblinks

New Brunswick Federation of Naturalists:

http://www.naturenb.ca/

The website of this non-profit, charitable organization helps New Brunswickers celebrate, conserve and protect New Brunswick's natural heritage.

The Nature Trust of New Brunswick

http://www.naturetrust.nb.ca/

The website of this organization tells you what is being done to preserve the province's diverse ecosystems, and welcomes you to get involved.

Irving Nature Park

http://new-brunswick.net/Saint_John/inp/

This website introduces a wonderful park located on the outskirts of Saint John. It features 200 km of trails from which one is apt to spy a number of coastal New Brunswick's animals and plants.

Government of NB, Department of Natural Resources

http://www.gnb.ca/0078/index-e.asp

This website, maintained by the provincial government, gives you the low-down on all things nature in New Brunswick.

Weather

There's a saying in the Maritimes – if you don't like the weather, wait five minutes. This adage has real meaning in New Brunswick, where weather conditions can vary widely from one region to another. Coastal areas boast fog and are comparatively temperate year round, while the central zones experience a wider range of temperature with colder winters and warmer summers.

RAIN

New Brunswick has the second most precipitation in Canada, receiving 1155.71 mm of precipitation annually, far greater than the national average of 522.14 mm. Only Nova Scotia gets more than New Brunswick.

New Brunswick also rates second after Nova Scotia in terms of rainfall. The province gets 854.73 mm of rain a year, more than twice the Canadian average of 345.24 mm.

New Brunswickers can expect to use their umbrellas 180.58 days a year, more than any Canadians except Newfoundlanders and Labradorians and Quebecers. Nationally, Canadians face an average of 145.44 rainy days.

Source: Environment Canada.

Take 5 — WEATHERMAN CLAUDE CÔTÉ'S
TOP FIVE NEW BRUNSWICK WEATHER STORIES

Claude Côté is a meteorologist with Environment Canada in Fredericton. He moved to the capital region in 1992 after five years in Newfoundland and Labrador. His background is in weather forecasting but in the past few years he has taken over the responsibility of weather preparedness and outreach meteorologist. Weather is not only his work; it's also his passion.

1. Snowy Moncton

On the last day of January 1992, a major winter storm was approaching from the southwest, a so-called 'bomb' development off the U.S. seaboard. Snow began in Moncton late in the evening of the 30th and by late afternoon on the 31st the visibility was less than one kilometer in snow and blowing snow, remaining so until the evening of February 2nd. One hundred and seventy centimeters of snow fell during that particular storm. As of today, February 1st still holds the record for maximum daily snowfall amount (measured at the Moncton airport) with 83 cm. Needless to say, the city was paralyzed for several days.

2. Foggy Saint John

There's no doubt that Saint John is the foggiest city in New Brunswick, but how foggy is it? Well, in July and August, for more than half of each month, fog is reported at the Saint John airport "17 and 16 days of fog, respectively, with visibility of less than half a mile". The foggiest month on record is July 1967, during which Saint John residents experienced 27 days of fog. When looking for the longest stretch of fog on record, July 13, 1972 takes the honour. The fog rolled into the Saint John airport on that day and the visibility remained reduced to half a mile or less for three consecutive days.

3. Storm Surge in Pointe-du-Chêne

On occasion, the combination of astronomical tide and weather conditions produces a swelling of the ocean called a storm surge. Such a situation occurred on the evening of January 21, 2000. A very intense low-pressure area approaching from the southwest generated strong northerly winds, resulting in a water level of 1.4m above predicted astronomical high tide. Many communities along the coastal Kent county and southeast New Brunswick experienced flooding. The community of Pointe-du-Chêne was cut off from the mainland for several hours.

4. Severe Summer Weather

In New Brunswick we are likely to experience 15 to 20 days with thundershower activity. Out of these days only the odd one will grow to become a severe thunderstorm producing hail, strong wind and a good downpour. Any chance of a tornado? Northwest areas are more likely to experience this type of event, on average one a year. However, the deadliest tornado east of Ontario occurred in Bouctouche on August 6, 1879 leaving 7 dead, 10 injuries, 25 families homeless and $100,000 damage.

5. Snowy New Brunswick

Cold winter temperatures and stormy northeasterlies combine to make New Brunswick the snowiest of the Maritime Provinces. Northwestern regions of the province generally receive 300 to 400 cm of snow annually. Due to thawing periods, evaporation and packing of the snow cover, the actual snow depth is less than the cumulative snowfall amounts. Nevertheless, record snow depth belongs to St. Leonard, with 164 cm reported in February 1997, and the runner up is Kedgwick, with 160 cm reported in March 1991. This is as white as it gets for "winter lovers".

OVER THE BANKS

Most of the year, the majestic St. John River winds its way calmly through its valley. In spring, however, the St. John River can transform into a raging torrent, destroying all in its path. Residents of the St. John River valley have long had to contend with springtime floods – at least 6 in the last century.

The worst flood, by far, occurred in the spring of 1973. Snow and weather conditions made perfect flood conditions. In late April the winter snow pack was high and on April 25 the river crested at an unusually high level. Two days later, a rainstorm brought 75 mm of rain and mild snow-melting temperatures. The St. John rose rapidly, and on April 29 and 30 it crested in Fredericton at 28.3 ft, 25 ft feet above its normal summer level.

People and livestock along the southern stretches of the river had to be evacuated. Countless basements were flooded and roads were washed out. In downtown Fredericton, the provincial legislature was closed and the historic Lord Beaverbrook Hotel was out of commission for several weeks. In all, 2,200 homes and 370 businesses suffered damages valued at $12 million. In 2006 dollars this would be a whopping $57 million.

SNOW

- Average annual snowfall in northwestern New Brunswick: 300-400 cm
- Average annual snowfall in eastern and southern sections: 200-300 cm

Source: Environment Canada.

Did you know...

that a major flood on the St. John River can be expected once every 70 years?

They Said It

"It breaks wind furiously – spits a little – but we continue to manage it."
— Loyalist Edward Winslow, likening the New Brunswick climate to a child.

PASS THE SHOVEL

Each year, 28 percent of the province's precipitation falls as snow and each year New Brunswickers have to contend with 10.25 days of heavy snow (days with more than 10 cm), the second highest number in Canada (second only to Newfoundland and Labrador). Blowing snow is a factor on 9.68 days – not bad considering that Canadians as a whole deal with an average 28.54 days of blowing snow. But lest New Brunswickers get too smug, it's worth noting that New Brunswick has the second snowiest spring in Canada (next to Newfoundland and Labrador); an average 91.11 cm of snow falls each spring.

Source: Environment Canada.

Take 5 KEITH DEGRACE'S FIVE
FAVOURITE SNOWMOBILE TRAILS

New Brunswick has learned to celebrate its long, snowy winters. In the late-1970s, Bathurst hotelier and avid snowmobiler Keith DeGrace became one of the pioneers in promoting northern New Brunswick's abundance of snow to Americans and Europeans. Today the groomed, well-equipped trails are a major tourist attraction and draw millions of dollars to the region each winter. More than 9,000 km of snowmobile trails criss-cross the province.

1. **Bathurst to Mount Carleton and Reilly Brook.**
2. **Edmundston to Campbellton, then down to Bathurst.**
3. **Grand Falls to Saint-Quentin.**
4. **Along the Acadian Peninsula, from Caraquet to Tracadie to Neguac.**
5. **The 140 mile loop from Bathurst up to Popple Depot and back.**

WINTER CHILL

By national standards, New Brunswick's winters aren't too harsh. For 24.92 days a year, the mercury does not rise above -20 °C. However, nine other provinces are colder than this and Canadians as a whole spend an average of 94.14 days bundled up on days colder than -20 °C.

Source: Environment Canada

SNOW COVER

On average, there is snow on the ground in New Brunswick for 130.67 days of the year. This can vary widely. Saint John has snow on the ground for a mere 59 days, while Edmundston has a whopping 160 days of snow cover.

Sources: Climates of Canada. Environment Canada

WHITE CHRISTMAS

The chance of a white Christmas is pretty good in New Brunswick. Of the cities, your odds are best in the capital where you have an 85 percent chance of having snow on the ground Christmas morning. In Moncton, there is a 74 percent chance and in coastal Saint John, a 65 percent chance.

Record setting Christmas day snowfalls

Fredericton	23.0 cm in 1997
Moncton	21.8 cm in 1970
Saint John	27.9 cm in 1961

Source: Environment Canada.

Did you know...

that freezing precipitation falls about 12 days a year in New Brunswick? Fredericton gets about 34 hours of freezing rain a year and Moncton, 59.

Source: Environment Canada.

CHRISTMAS 1980

New Brunswickers really enjoyed their Yule logs on December 25th, 1980, the coldest Christmas on record for the province. Saint John's temperature peaked that day at just a -28.2°C, the coldest Christmas day since 1872. It was cold everywhere else, too. Woodstock, the coldest spot in the province, bottomed out at -31°C on Boxing Day. Fredericton weighed in at -28°C, Moncton at -27°C, Charlo at -26°C and Chatham at -28° C.

Source: Environment Canada.

IN A FOG

The Fundy coast is the foggiest place in the province, and, indeed, in the world. The summer months, when the air is warmest over the cold Atlantic, is the foggiest time of year.

PEA SOUP, ANYONE?

Saint John is the foggiest city in the province; only Newfoundland and Labrador's Grand Banks are foggier. The "Port city" is fogged in 25 percent of the time. In July, its foggiest month, the city is shrouded in fog 36 percent of the time. Mornings are the foggiest times of day– Saint Johners have to drive to work in the fog 60 percent of the time. But by their 2 p.m. coffee breaks, fog is an issue only 18 percent of the time. It's not just the visibility locals complain about – at times the temperature in foggy uptown Saint John can be 20°C lower than that at the fogless airport, 15 km inland.

Did you know...

that in the average December, Saint John is the sunniest spot in Eastern Canada with more that 100 hours of bright sunshine? Unfortunately, in July it ranks last.

- Elsewhere fog is less common, the fall months being foggiest season.

Miramichi	44 days
Campbellton	24 days
Moncton	60 days

- Apart from the Fundy coast, New Brunswick's incidence of fog is not exceptional. By way of comparison, Toronto has 35 fog days and Vancouver, 45.

Source: Environment Canada.

HEAT

New Brunswick has an average summer temperature of 23.28°C, the hottest average in Canada. Annually, the province has six days a year when temperatures exceed 30°C, second only to Saskatchewan. It also has the most humidex days above 30°C, with 25.06 in total. The province also claims title to the most smoke and haze days, numbering 22.16 each summer.

Average seasonal highs

January	-9.2
May	10.8
July	26.0
October	7.5

Source: Environment Canada; Government of New Brunswick.

They Said It

"*Sometimes out on the Bay of Fundy when the fog comes in thick you can sit on the boat's rail and lean your back up against it. So that's pretty thick fog out there; but you gotta be careful 'cause if the fog lifts quick you'll fall overboard*"
— **A New Brunswick tall tale recounted in** *The Climates of Canada*

SUNSHINE

Across New Brunswick there are between 140 and 160 sunny days each year, and 75 sunless days. The province has the sunniest winters in Canada, with 347.5 hours of sun each winter. It has the second sunniest falls at 405.73 hours; only Nova Scotia has more.

Source: Environment Canada.

WIND

Winds are light in New Brunswick on 258.35 days of the year. In winter, wind speeds average 14.72 km/h but the annual average wind speed recorded in the province is 13.6 km/h. Winds tend to be lightest inland, while the seacoast is breezier.

The windiest city is Moncton, where average annual wind speeds are 16.62 km/h. Saint John places second with winds of 16.05 km/h, Bathurst ranks third with winds of 13.4 km/h and Fredericton is the least windy city with average annual winds of 12.38 km/h.

Source: Environment Canada.

LIGHTNING

In New Brunswick each year there are an average 14.65 days on which there are thunder and lightning storms. Each year the capital city sees 50 strikes of lightning, a far cry from the 251 strikes reported in Canada's most "electric city," Windsor, ON, but considerably more than the one lightning strike recorded annually in Inuvik.

Source: Environment Canada.

Did you know...

that when the Loyalists first arrived in the Bay of Fundy, they spent two weeks stranded off shore, unable to find Saint John through a damp curtain of fog?

TORNADOES

Tornadoes are rare in New Brunswick. When they do happen they tend to be minor, such as those twisters which caused some excitement in Carleton County in July 2006, but did relatively little damage. An exception to the rule occurred on August 6, 1879. That day a tornado ripped through the village of Buctouche leaving 7 dead, 10 injured and 25 families homeless.

Source: Environment Canada.

AND THE WINNER IS . . .

- Highest recorded temperature: 39.4°C, Nepisiguit Falls, Rexton, and Woodstock on August 18 and 19, 1935
- Lowest recorded temperature: -47.2°C, Sisson Dam, a weather station near Plaster Rock, on February 1, 1955
- Snowiest winter: 704 cm of snow fell at Tide Head, 1954-55
- Highest recorded rainfall: 2,150 mm at Alma in 1979.
- Highest recorded wind gust: 137 km/h at Miscou Island, October 21, 1968
- Most fog days in a single year: 127 days, at the Saint John Airport in 1971
- Longest wet period: 208 wet days at Tide Head in 1954
- Snowiest city: Campbellton where an averages 392 cm falls each year
- Rainiest city: Saint John, which averages 1147.9 mm a year
- Warmest City: Moncton/Dieppe, with an annual average temperature of 5.8°C

Source: Environment Canada.

Did you know...

that 90 percent of the smog that occurs in Atlantic Canada happens in southern New Brunswick and south-western Nova Scotia, the Bay of Fundy and Saint John areas?

GROWING SEASON

- Average last frost

Edmundston	May 28
Saint John	May 2

- Average first frost

Edmundston	September 18
Saint John	October 21

- Longest frost-free period, Grand Manan 204 days, recorded in 1902

Source: Environment Canada.

HARNESSING THE WEATHER

Although New Brunswick has fought hard to shed the nickname the "drive through province," it wouldn't mind being known as the "blow-through province" and is actively encouraging the development of wind power. Plans are in the works to allow businesses and individuals to harness wind power and sell the excess back to the energy grid.

Any kilowatt-hours generated by wind power are to be subtracted from the kilowatt-hours obtained from NB Power. By 2010, New Brunswick hopes to acquire 100MW of power from renewable energy projects, including wind power, and by 2016 a third of all energy consumed in the province will come from renewable sources. Five regions are being proposed for wind development: the Bay of Fundy, Tantramar, Miramichi Bay, Acadie-Chaleur and inland New Brunswick.

TIDAL POWER

New Brunswick is behind Nova Scotia when it comes to harnessing the power of the world famous Fundy tides. A 2006 study proposes that it will be at least a decade before tidal power becomes a reality in the province. Nevertheless, there are high hopes that a plant in Head Harbour Passage, between Deer Island and Campobello Island, could generate enough electricity to power between 4,500 and 12,000 homes.

SNOW DAY, ERR . . . WEEK

Thanks to its location near the Bay of Fundy, Moncton gets more than its fair share of snowstorms. But a 110-hour blizzard in early February 1992 was exceptional even by Moncton's snowy standards. The storm brought wind gusts of 140 km/h and a record snowfall of 163 cm. Extreme drifting made driving hazardous and many motorists had to be rescued from their stranded cars.

The city came to a standstill and for a week schools and businesses kept their doors closed. On Main Street, some stores managed to open that week, but they were forced to spray paint the names of their businesses in the snow as their signs were buried. The also has to carve "snow doors" though giant banks to allow customers to enter their establishments.

ESCUMINAC DISASTER

Early in the evening of Friday June 19, 1959, 54 fishing boats left the small Acadian coastal community of Escuminac intending to set their salmon nets before nightfall. The 5 p.m. weather forecast called for a calm evening, but at 8:45 p.m. a storm warning was issued. The surprise storm, an extra tropical event, had been a hurricane earlier that day.

It had been expected to turn out to sea, but took a surprise westward turn into the Gulf of St. Lawrence. The storm warning came too late. Described by witnesses as the worst storm they had seen, it churned up 50 and 60 foot waves. The small Escuminac fishing boats were no match and the terrified fishers who survived described their

Did you know...

that weather phenomenon are not the only things to appear in New Brunswick skies? UFOs have also been sighted. In one such case, in June 1992, army reservists training in woods near Gagetown reported seeing an oval or round aircraft, covered in three sets of lights, hovering above the tree line.

time on the angry sea as "two days and nights of terror." For days following the storm the horrified community watched boat fragments wash up on shore. In all, 22 boats were lost, taking 35 men and boys with them.

WATCH THAT SHADOW

Anyone living in southern New Brunswick on February 2, 1976 will never forget the "Groundhog Day Gale." One of the fiercest storms in the history of the Maritimes, it slammed into Saint John with particular ferocity bringing winds of 188 km/h, 12 m waves and 10 m swells. Salt spray coated the landscape for miles inland.

Coastal zones were particularly hard hit as vicious seas eroded huge chunks of shoreline. The storm did tens of millions of dollars of damage; everything from docks, to homes, boats and utility poles fell victim to the gale.

The storm had another significant consequence. As a result of the powerful winds, many breeds of seabirds disappeared and have never returned. As if the storm itself wasn't bad enough, a wave of bitterly cold Arctic air swept into the province in its aftermath. This added to the cleanup challenge and caused countless broken water lines.

SAXBY GALE

In 1868, Lieutenant Saxby of the Royal Navy sent a letter to several British newspapers predicting that an intense storm and exceptional tides would occur at seven o'clock on the morning of October 5, 1869. Saxby's prediction was no mere hunch. An accomplished sailor, he knew that on that date the weather would be influenced both by a new moon and the fact that the moon would on that day make its monthly passage closest to Earth.

Few paid attention to Saxby's warnings, but he was right. Late in the afternoon of October 4, 1869, a hurricane-velocity storm struck the Bay of Fundy. At Saint John, heavy waves pounded ships against the wharves and virtually all communities around the Bay of Fundy were flooded. In Moncton, the tide rose nearly 2 m above former records. Property damage was substantial.

At St. Andrews, 123 boats were washed ashore. On Campobello Island, more than 80 buildings were destroyed. Church steeples across the province succumbed, roofs were blown off and telegraph poles snapped like twigs. More than 70 lives were lost to the storm.

A cemetery at Hillsborough, the final resting place of many victims,

Take 5 FIVE HORRIBLE HURRICANES

1.**Galveston Hurricane**, 1900.
Known more for the devastation it caused in the Texas town from which it takes its name, this storm passed through the Gaspé and northern New Brunswick, bringing high winds and dumping 64 mm of rain on Bathurst. Its damage was compounded by the fact that tides were unusually high that day. Eight fishing boats and 38 crewmembers out of Gloucester County were lost.

2. **Hurricane Edna**, September, 1954.
Although no lives were lost when Edna smashed through New Brunswick, damage and flooding were extensive.

3. **Unnamed hurricane**, 1959.
The fact that this storm had no name did not diminish its fury. Thirty-three lobster fisherman were killed as winds reached 120 km/hr.

4. **Hurricane Belle**,1976.
Belle caused substantial flooding across the province when she made her presence felt in August.

5. **Hurricane Bob**,1991
After leaving Cape Cod, Bob hit southern New Brunswick with winds of 100 km/hr. Bob killed 2.

offers a sober reminder of the storm's ferocity. Many of these deceased were farmers. Fearful of loosing their herds, they had gone down to the marshes to lead their livestock home. Tragically, the dykes holding back the sea broke, and these men and their animals were swept away.

PLEISTOCENE PARK

When glaciers receded from Atlantic Canada more than 10,000 years ago, a warmer more temperate climate was ushered in. On the cliffs overlooking the Bay of Fundy in Fundy National Park, however, the conditions have remained so dreary and inhospitable that Arctic plants such as the Primula laurentiana (Bird's Eye Primrose) still grow, remnants of the Pleistocene age when glaciers covered the province.

Weblinks

Weather Winners
http://www.on.ec.gc.ca/weather/winners/
Find out how New Brunswick's weather conditions stack up against other places in Canada at this website maintained by Environment Canada.

Weather Conditions
http://www.weatheroffice.ec.gc.ca/forecast/canada/index_e.html?id=NB
Want to know what the weather is like right now in New Brunswick? Check this Environment Canada website out.

Snowmobiling
http://www.nbfsc.com/eindex.html
Want to know more about how to enjoy New Brunswick's wintry weather? Visit this website maintained by the New Brunswick Federation of Snowmobile Clubs.

NEW BRUNSWICK

1867

Politics

POLITICAL BEGINNINGS

In 1763, New Brunswick was known as Sunbury County, part of the large colony of Nova Scotia. It was ruled from Halifax, but that all changed in 1783 when thousands of Loyalists landed in Sunbury County. They simply would not tolerate being shut out of the political establishment.

Immediately, they began to clamour for the creation of a Loyalist province, a province that would return them to the leadership roles they had enjoyed in the 13 colonies. They wanted a province that would, as Loyalist leader Edward Winslow proclaimed, become "the envy of the American States."

In 1784, the Loyalists got their wish when the colony of New Brunswick was created. The government of the new colony featured an elected assembly (charged with spending British money in the colony) and the appointed Legislative Council that, not surprisingly, came to be dominated by Loyalist elites. The former Acadian town of Ste. Anne was renamed Fredericton and made the capital.

POLITICS AND PINE TREES

The all-important timber trade shaped early New Brunswick's politics. The Commissioner of Crown lands (who was in charge of the timber stands) wielded so much power in the colony that he was considered second in charge to the governor.

In the 1830s, Thomas Baillie held this position. By charging taxes on felled trees, Baillie was able to raise large amounts of money, which, in the pre-democratic era, was controlled by the appointed Legislative Council, not the elected assembly.

This meant the Council could operate while paying heed neither to the wishes of elected assemblymen nor the New Brunswickers who voted for them. This became more than just a minor annoyance for the assembly and the public. After much lobbying, in 1837 the assembly was finally granted the right to control colonial money and determine how it would be spent.

RESPONSIBLE GOVERNMENT

In the 1840s, Britain voiced interest in setting her North American holdings free as independent self-governing colonies. The newly empowered New Brunswick assembly, still chaffing under the inordinate control wielded by the appointed legislative council, could not agree more. In 1848 Nova Scotia won responsible government, in 1851 PEI, and New Brunswick followed in their footsteps a few years later, in 1854.

THE COMING OF CONFEDERATION

As an independent colony, New Brunswick fared well. And so, when the colonies of Upper and Lower Canada began to talk Confederation in 1864, New Brunswick's support was, at best, lukewarm. Samuel Leonard

They Said It

"O! patronage! patronage! It is that which constitutes the whole power of the Executive Government of this Province; and when the future historian of New Brunswick records the history of these times, he may sum up the whole duties of the Executive in these words."
— Speech of Loyalist-bred New Brunswick politician, Lemuel A. Wilmot, 1847

Take 5 ARTHUR DOYLE'S FIVE MOST
MEMORABLE NEW BRUNSWICK
POLITICAL SCANDALS

Arthur Doyle is a Fredericton political historian and author of Front Benches & Back Rooms: A story of corruption, muckraking, raw partisanship, and intrigue in New Brunswick.

1. Charges against Premier Richard Hatfield for possession of marijuana were laid in 1984. Police reported that they found a small package of the drug in the Premier's suitcase before it was loaded on the plane of the visiting Queen Elizabeth. He was later acquitted of the charges.

2. The Bricklin automobile company, heavily financed by Hatfield's provincial government, was placed in receivership in 1975. The failed venture cost New Brunswick taxpayers over $20 million. The federal government also lost $2 million

3. The Westmorland Chemical Park's ammonium nitrate plant, the Robichaud Government's star industrial development initiative, closed after announcing $12 million in operating losses in 1967. The loss was underwritten by the New Brunswick taxpayers. Another $15 million was lost in infrastructure investments, which included a 'floating dock'.

4. Premier James Kidd Flemming was forced to resign as premier in 1914 when a Royal Commission found that he was aware of improper fund raising activities involving lumber companies and his chief party fund raiser. Flemming was subsequently elected a Member of Parliament.

5. The Patriotic Potato scandal was exposed in 1919. During WWI the provincial Conservative government financed the purchase of 150,000 thousand barrels of potatoes from New Brunswick farmers to donate to refugees in war torn Europe. A three-year Royal Commission investigation uncovered a tale of rampant patronage, kickbacks, misappropriation of government funds and perjury. Thousands of barrels of potatoes rotted on the docks in Saint John while a number of government friends filled their pockets.

"I propose that any government of which I am the head will at the first session of parliament initiate whatever action is necessary to that end, or perish in the attempt."

— Prime Minister R.B. Bennett, June 9, 1930, on the elimination of unemployment. He wasn't very successful. When car owners during the depression could not afford to buy gasoline, they harnessed teams of horses or oxen to their cars in order to pull them around. The name of this improvisation? Bennett Buggies.

Tilley led the Confederation forces, but his plans were scuttled when he lost the 1865 provincial election to anti-Confederate, Albert Smith.

New Brunswickers feared the economic consequences of union, and believed that a free trade deal with the United States, not union with other colonies, was what would secure its fortunes. The Smith government was short-lived and Confederation was again the main issue in the election of 1866.

Less than a week before the election Tilley's camp got the break it needed. A rag-taggle group of five Fenians, expatriate Irish Catholics who wanted British North America annexed to the United States, 'invaded' New Brunswick and planted a flag on Campobello Island. The failure of renewed free trade with the U.S., coupled with the perceived Fenian threat, inspired New Brunswickers to cast their ballots for Tilley and Confederation.

Did you know...

that Jean Chrétien, named federal Liberal leader in June 1990, earned his ticket to the House of Commons that December by winning a by-election in Beauséjour, NB? Romeo LeBlanc stepped down to allow the Prime Minister to run in his riding. Chrétien later named LeBlanc Governor General.

They Said It

"Had we not had Louis, had we not had the 1960s, I don't know where we would be today. We would probably be anglicized, marginalized, hunting for a soul."

— **Donald Savoie, professor of public administration at the University of Moncton, in a CBC interview**

POLITICAL GEOGRAPHY
Municipalities
- 7 cities
- 28 towns
- 68 villages
- 272 local service districts (to administer areas of sparse population)

Source: Government of New Brunswick.

ON THE FEDERAL SCENE
Just one New Brunswicker has been Prime Minister of Canada. Conservative Richard Bedford Bennett held the nation's highest elected office from 1930-1935. Prime Minister during the depths of the Great Depression, he was much blamed for government policies that failed to rescue Canadians from their despair. He was so unpopular that he chose to live out his final days in England.

PROVINCIAL POLITICS
- Provincial ridings/MLAs: 55
- Location of legislature: Queen Street, downtown Fredericton

Did you know...

that Rexton's Andrew Bonar Law is the only person born outside of the British Isles to serve as Prime Minister of Great Britain? He held that office from 1922-23.

Bio RICHARD HATFIELD

Picture this: Conservative premier Richard Hatfield proudly posing behind the wheel of his gull-winged, New Brunswick-built Bricklin sportster. This image seems to capture the essence of this most controversial of premiers. He was a Studio 54 regular, a party-going bachelor willing to take risks to drag the province into the modern era, whether it liked it or not.

Hatfield entered politics in 1961 and won the premiership in 1970. His first order of business was to continue Louis J. Robichaud's program of making New Brunswick the only officially bilingual province. Although he never mastered the French language himself, Hatfield was widely popular among Acadians.

Under his watch, provincial arts and culture were showered with unprecedented attention. Although he battled hard to lift the sagging economic fortunes of the 'have-not' province, his loss of $23-million in the ill-fated Bricklin fiasco won him scorn and became fodder for countless jokes. And yet, it reflected his unwavering belief that the New Brunswick economy needed to be modernized and diversified

On the national scene, he emerged as a leader in constitutional issues, playing pivotal roles in patriating the Constitution, developing the Charter of Rights, and in the failed effort to pass the Meech Lake Accord. Interested in constitutional affairs, he also worked tirelessly to ensure that New Brunswick got its dues when it came to economic development.

Unfortunately, Hatfield's personal life and foibles overshadowed political accomplishments. His wanderlust saw him constantly out of the province and rumours of inappropriate behavior culminated with his 1984 arrest for possession of marijuana while boarding Queen Elizabeth's private plane. By then, the people had had enough of 'Disco Dick'. He hung on as leader until Frank McKenna's Liberals handed him a humiliating defeat by winning every single seat in the province in 1987. He died four years later of brain cancer.

Did you know...

that from 1960 until today, all New Brunswick premiers have been elected to that office before their fortieth birthdays?

FEDERAL FACTS

- Voting districts: 10
- Members of Parliament: 10
- Senators: 10

Source: Government of New Brunswick.

FRANCHISE FACTS

- Requisites to vote: 18 years of age; resident in the province for six months
- First elected assembly: 1784
- Responsible government: 1854

PREMIER PRIMER

New Brunswick's first premier, the man who took New Brunswick into Confederation, was A.R. Wetmore, leader of the Confederation Party. Since Wetmore, there have been 30 premiers, 15 Liberal and 15 Conservative.

Take 5 TOP FIVE YOUNGEST PREMIERS OF NEW BRUNSWICK.

1. George King – 29
2. Bernard Lord – 33
3. Louis J. Robichaud – 35
4. Frank McKenna – 36
5. Shawn Graham – 38

"They shall have Dominion from sea to sea."
Psalms 72:8

— Pro-confederate New Brunswicker Leonard Tilley
offering his Biblical spin on Confederation

FIRST ACADIAN

The first Acadian premier was Peter J. Veniot. When Liberal Premier Walter Foster resigned in 1923, Veniot was selected to assume the reigns of government. Veniot lost the 1925 provincial election to Conservative John Baxter. Louis Robichaud was the first Acadian premier elect.

MPS CURRENTLY IN OTTAWA

- 6 Liberal MPs
- 3 Conservative MPs
- 1 NDP MP
- 0 Green Party MPs
- 0 female MPs

Source: Elections Canada

CONFEDERATION OF REGIONS

In the 1980s a new political player arrived on the scene in New Brunswick. Tapping into New Brunswickers' dissatisfaction with the scandal-plagued 1980s Liberals, the Confederation of Region's (CoR) party won 4.3 percent of votes cast in its inaugural 1988 bid. Running

They Said It

"The best social program we have is a job."

— Frank McKenna

Take 5

FIVE CAREERS OF
NEW BRUNSWICK PREMIERS BEFORE THEY WERE ELECTED

1. **James Kidd Flemming:** traveling salesman
2. **George J. Clarke:** newspaper editor
3. **John Baxter:** butcher's accountant
4. **P.J. Veniot:** journalist and typographer
5. **Bernard Lord:** car salesman

on a platform that included a promise to repeal the 1969 Official Languages Act, CoR gained most of its support in Anglophone regions.

In 1991, it parlayed votes into seats, winning 21.2 percent of the vote and capturing eight seats, enough to form the official opposition. Leadership squabbles and infighting tested the party in the early 1990s and party membership plummeted from 20,000 to 5,000. In the 1995 election, CoR won just 7.1 percent of the popular vote and had no members elected. The party was dissolved in 2002.

ACADIANS IN POLITICS

For generations Acadians in New Brunswick were shut out of politics. They have nevertheless made their marks in provincial and national politics.

- Until 1810 Acadians could not vote by virtue of their Catholicism.
- Until 1830 Catholic Acadians could not run for office.
- The first Acadian was not elected to the colonial assembly until 1846.

Did you know...

that although the election results of 1987 were totally one-sided (the Liberals won all seats), 39.1 percent of voters actually cast their ballots for the opposition?

- In 1867, Auguste Renaud, a Liberal from Kent, was the first Acadian to sit in the House of Commons.
- In 1885, Pascal Porier became the first Acadian Senator.
- In 1960, Louis Robichaud becamethe first elected Acadian premier.
- In 1971, Hédard Joseph Robichaud was named the first Lieutenant Governor.
- In 1987, Aldea Landry was the first Acadian woman elected to the New Brunswick assembly.

Bio FRANK MCKENNA

"The government of the United States is in large measure dysfunctional." Ouch. These are pretty harsh words from Canada's Ambassador to the United States, a guy raised on a farm in tiny Apohaqui, near Sussex. But Frank McKenna has always been inclined to call 'em as he sees 'em.

A celebrated trial lawyer, provincial cheerleader and business bigwig, McKenna has been on the national political radar for almost thirty years. Although some dispute the 'McKenna Miracle' — the apparent lifting of the province's fortunes thanks to his premiership of 1987 to 1997 — none can deny the respect he commands on the national political stage.

In his inaugural bid for the premier's chair, the whole of New Brunswick went Liberal red for the first time in history. In fact, one of his biggest challenges was to create a voice for alterative views in the Legislature in the absence of an official opposition (he implemented a Liberal 'unofficial opposition' for this purpose).

His second bid for the premiership in 1991 saw his Liberals opposed by the Coalition of Regions Party, a short-lived rag-tag party built precariously on an anti-bilingualism platform. With no effectual opposition in the Legislature, McKenna set about putting people to work.

- Pierrette Ringuette of Madaswaska became the first Acadian woman to be elected to the House of Common in 1993.
- In 1994, Roméo LeBlanc became the first Acadian Governor General.
- In 1995, Rose-Marie Losier-Cool was the first Acadian woman from the Maritimes appointed to the Senate.

Did you know...

that the secret ballot was not introduced to New Brunswick until 1855?

For good or bad, McKenna measured his success as premier against a yardstick of employment statistics. McKenna took Canada's first foray into 'workfare' when he compelled welfare recipients to cut brush for their tiny cheques. He also wooed multinationals, enticing them to establish the now-ubiquitous call-centres.

His shrewd business approach to politics did not go unnoticed and when he left office he easily moved into the corporate world, serving on several major boards and eventually becoming chairman of CanWest Global. His 2005 appointment as ambassador to the U.S. fueled rumours of his pending bid for the leadership of the federal Liberals. These rumours seemed veritably confirmed when he resigned this post shortly after Martin's Liberals lost the 2006 election.

McKenna had other plans. The New Brunswick politician, well known for being at his desk before seven every morning, informed shocked Canadians that he would not be seeking the Liberal leadership. He had, he said, already made enough personal sacrifices for the sake of politics. Many find it hard to believe that this driven politician is truly done with politics. Only time will tell.

Take 5 ROBERT PICHETTE'S TOP FIVE
ACADIAN POLITICAL LEADERS

Robert Pichette, a Moncton author and journalist, was Executive Assistant and Deputy Minister under Premier Louis J. Robichaud during the 1960s. His latest book is Le pays appel L'Acadie: essais sur des commemorations acadiennes.

1. Marcel-Francois Richard (1847-1915), founded Rogersville, a college, built fourteen churches, two monasteries, several convents and some fifty schools. The fiercely nationalist priest was instrumental in forcing the Vatican to appoint the first Acadian Bishop in New Brunswick. He was responsible, in 1884, for the adoption of the Acadian symbols, including the flag. At his death, he was hailed unanimously, and rightly, as 'Father of the Nation' and 'Apostle of the Acadian Renaissance'.

2. Pascal Poirier (1852-1933), the first Acadian Senator, a jurist and an eminent writer, he was elected to the Royal Society of Canada. Poirier worked tirelessly, and successfully, for the promotion of the Acadian people at all levels. He was President of the National Society of the Acadians, and France made him a Knight of the Legion of Honour.

3. Louis J. Robichaud (1925-2005), was a visionary Premier of New Brunswick for ten years in the 1960s, during which he changed the governance system of the province at every level with his revolution-ary Equal Opportunity Program. The first Acadian premier, Robichaud introduced official bilingualism to the province and gave it its flag among many initiatives. He later served in the Senate where he was assiduous. He was made a Companion of the Order of Canada, the order's highest level, and a Commander of France's Legion of Honour.

4. Clément Cormier (1910-1987), as much a visionary and as determined as his friend Louis J. Robichaud, was an outstanding educator. The last president of Saint Joseph's University became the founder and first president of the Université de Moncton and, later, its Chancellor. There was not a single Acadian initiative going on during his active life in which he was not involved in some way. Vincent Massey, then Chairman of the Royal Commission on National Development in the Arts, Letters and Sciences (1949), said if he were asked to name the twenty greatest living Canadians he would "undoubtedly list the Rev. Father Cormier, St. Joseph's capable, popular and scholarly president and later the President of the New Brunswick Museum." Cormier was awarded the rank of Companion of the Order of Canada.

5. Bella Léger (1899-1995), blazed new trails for women in New Brunswick and elsewhere. An outstanding educator, she joined the Sisters of Charity of Saint John but left with other Acadian nuns in 1924 to found the Sisters of Our Lady of the Sacred Heart in Moncton. In 1936, she studied at the world-famous Sorbonne in Paris, which was extremely rare , if not a first for a nun and a woman from Kent County! She became the first Acadian woman to obtain a certificate of French teaching from a French university. A visionary and a most capable administrator, she was one of the foundresses and the first Superior of College Notre-Dame d'Acadie, a women's college in Moncton whose influence was felt in several North and Latin American countries. In 1954, she was elected Superior General of her congregation and is an Officer of the Order of Canada.

They Said It

NOTABLE POLITICAL WOMEN

Frances Fish: First to run for elected provincial office (1935)

Brenda Roberston: First to win a provincial seat (1967)

Muriel McQueen Fergusson: First female senator from Atlantic Canada, 1953

Marion Upton: First female mayor in a New Brunswick municipality, 1967 (Minto)

Brenda Robertson: First woman elected to NB assembly, 1967 (Conservative)

Shirley Dysart: The first female Liberal elected to the New Brunswick Legislative Assembly, 1974

Elsie Wayne: First female mayor of Saint John, 1983

Elizabeth Weir: First female leader of a political party, 1988 (NDP)

Barbara Baird: First woman Leader of the Progressive Conservative Party of New Brunswick, 1989

They Said It

Did you know...

that when New Brunswick Senator David Wark died in office in 1905 he was 101 years old?

Elizabeth Weir: First elected female leader of the provincial NDP, 1991
Shirley Dysart: First woman speaker in the Legislature, 1991
Honourable Margaret Norrie McCain: First female Lieutenant-Governor, 1994

Weblinks

These websites, maintained by the various political parties, provide information on their platforms, candidates and party events.
The Progressive Conservative Party Homepage
http://www.pcnb.org

New Brunswick Liberal Party
http://www.nbliberal.ca/index.htm

The New Brunswick New Democratic Party
http://www.ndp-npd.nb.ca/index-e.html

Canadian Confederation, New Brunswick
http://www.collectionscanada.ca/confederation/023001-2110-e.html
Learn all about New Brunswick and Confederation with this website maintained by the federal government of Canada.

Legislative Assembly of New Brunswick
http://www.gnb.ca/legis/index-e.asp
Want to know what's going on in government? Check out this website which features a live webcam of happenings in the Legislative Assembly.

Then and Now

POPULATION, THEN AND NOW

- 1784   12,000
- 1840   156,162
- 1851   193,800
- 1901   331,120
- 1951   515,697
- 2001   729,498
- 2005   752,006

Sources: Statistics Canada; NB Dept of Vital Statistics, NB Dept of Finance.

PERCENTAGE RURAL/URBAN DIVIDE, THEN AND NOW

	Urban	Rural
1851	14	86
1901	23	77
1951	42	58

Did you know...

that before it was created in 1784, all of New Brunswick was
known as Sunbury County, part of Nova Scotia?

1966	51	49 (first year that the majority lived in cities)
1971	57	43 (year of highest relative urban population)
1991	48	52
2001	50	50

Source: Statistics Canada

POPULATION DENSITY: PEOPLE/ KM^2

	New Brunswick	Canada
1871	4.02	0.41
1901	4.61	0.6
1951	7.25	1.5
2001	10.6	3.3

LIFE EXPECTANCY

	Men	Women
1951	65.9	69.8
2001	76.1	81.9

Between 1951 and 1991, the life expectancy of New Brunswickers increased by 9.74 years, with women gaining more than men (11.06 years vs. 8.32 years). Nationally, life expectancy rose by 9.29 years during the same period.

Sources: Statistics Canada; Source Canadian Council on Social Development.

ACADIAN POPULATION
(PERCENTAGE OF PROVINCIAL POPULATION)

1901	79,979 (24 percent)
1951	185,110 (35.9 percent)
2001	242,070 (33.6 percent)

Source: Francophone and Acadian Community Profile.

STRENGTH THROUGH UNITY

The first Acadians to settle in New Brunswick lived at Ste. Anne, modern day Fredericton. By 1755, the year of the deportation, 2,300 Acadians lived in the St. John River valley. With the deportation, Ste. Anne was burned to the ground. Residents were exiled, but a few managed to escape, and hide in the woods for several years, thanks to their Maliseet neighbours.

In 1764, when the Acadians were permitted to return, they found Ste. Anne occupied by British settlers and so they moved on, settling the St. John River above Ste. Anne and in the Kennebecasis River valley.

The Loyalist influx of 1783 marked another turning point in Acadians' lives. Faced with Loyalist competition for land, and offered no protection, the Acadians were forced to move yet again. In 1785, 24 dispossessed Acadian families petitioned for and were granted 200-acre land grants north of Edmundston, in an area called 'the Madawaska'.

Here they finally found their first permanent home in New Brunswick. It was from here in the 19th century that Acadian culture experienced a resurgence, fuelled by enhanced educational opportunities and a growing population. The 1847 publication of Henry Wadsworth Longfellow's popular epic poem, *Evangeline, A Tale of Acadie*, and its 1865 translation into French, also fuelled this renaissance.

In 1881, Acadian leaders held a National Convention in Memramcook, where they chose their National Holiday (August 15) and patron saint (the Virgin Mary). Three years later, Acadians chose their national flag (the Tricolour), national anthem (Ave Maris Stella), motto (strength through unity) and badge (featuring a star with rays and the motto).

Did you know...

that Winnifred Blair of Saint John was crowned the very first Miss Canada in 1923?

PLACE NAMES, THEN AND NOW

Then	Now
Ste. Anne	Fredericton
Nepisiguit/St. Peters	Bathurst
Buttermill Creek	Florenceville
Petit-Sault	Edmundston
Ebaghuit/ Great Island of the Passamoquoddy	Campobello Island
Salmon River	Plumsweep
Magaguadavic/ Granite Town	St.George
Peabody	Maugerville
Wordens	Evandale
Parrtown	Saint John
Munquart	Bath

WOMEN AND POLITICS, THEN AND NOW

In 1849, the New Brunswick government legislated that women could neither vote nor hold public office. In subsequent decades New Brunswick women joined their sisters across North America in calling for the right to vote and in 1894 the Women's Enfranchisement Association was established in Saint John.

It took a while, but in April 1919 women received the right to vote. This was just a partial victory, because it wasn't until 1934 that women could hold office. A year later Frances Fish became the first woman to run for provincial office, though it would be another 32 years before Brenda Robertson would be the first woman provincially elected.

Other restrictions hampered the ability of women to participate in the political system. Until the 1960s, many homemakers were disqual-

Did you know...

that in December 2003, Ottawa adopted a Royal Proclamation declaring each July 28 a Day of Commemoration for the Great Upheaval (the Acadian Deportation of 1755-1763)?

They Said It

"... *your petitioners humbly pray that lands proportioned to the number of their families may be granted to them and their children at a place called the Madawaska, between the Seven Islands and the River de Vert (Green River) on the River St-John.*"
—**1785 Petition of Acadians to Governor Carleton**

ified from voting because only taxpayers had the right. It was only in 1966 that age and residency became the only voting criteria.

Today, the law doesn't prevent women from holding public office, but something seems to be. Currently, fewer than 13 percent of the province's Members of the Legislative Assembly are women. Only 25 percent of city councillors are female as are a mere 13 percent of the province's mayors. New Brunswick has no female Members of Parliament.

FARMING TRANSFORMATION

In the twentieth century, the New Brunswick family farm gave way to 'factory farms.' Fewer, but larger, more efficiently managed and corporately-owned farms are now typical of rural New Brunswick. Between 1951 and 1991, the province lost 87.7 percent of its farms (nationally, the loss was 55.1 percent). The farm population also plummeted, by 97.7 percent (nationally, the loss was 70.3 percent).

Source: Canadian Journal of Regional Science.

NUMBER OF FARMS IN NEW BRUNSWICK
1951   26,431
2001   3,034

NUMBER OF MEN EMPLOYED ON FARMS
1891   50,275
1911   44,840
1951   22,977
2002   8,010

Did you know...

that in the nineteenth century, New Brunswick communities auctioned off the poor to the person who agreed to care for that person for the lowest amount of tax money? The purchased pauper would be required to assist the successful bidder around the house and farm.

ACRES OF FARM HOLDINGS IN NEW BRUNSWICK

1871	3,828,000
1901	4,443,000
1951	3,479,000
2001	958,899

TOTAL NET FARM INCOME

1926:	$16,892,000
1951:	$28,330,000
2001:	$412,606,000

Source: Statistics Canada.

EDUCATION

Soon after their arrival, the Loyalists raised the call for free public education. In 1871 the Common Free School Act made this a reality. Until the 1950s, most New Brunswickers were educated in one room schoolhouses, and by 1900 the province had 1,600 of them.

In the 1950s and 60s, with the coming of paved roads, school busses and Louis Robichaud's Equal Opportunity policy, larger consolidated schools replaced the one-roomed school. In 1981, New Brunswickers were guaranteed education in both official languages. In the 1990s, the education system was reformed again. Kindergarten became a provincial offering and the number of school districts was reduced to 18. Five years later, school boards were disbanded, replaced with parent advisory groups at the school and district levels.

NUMBER OF CHILDREN ENROLLED IN PUBLIC OR ELEMENTARY SCHOOLS IN NEW BRUNSWICK

1867 31,000 (percentage who attended on a daily basis: 47.1)
1900 67,000 (56.2 percent)
1950 106,000 (80.3 percent)
2001 129,129

Source: Statistics Canada.

HIGHER EDUCATION

New Brunswick has four public universities, which range in age from 43 to 212 years old.

- The University of New Brunswick, originally called King's College, was established in 1784. It is the first public university in North America and is the oldest English-language university in Canada.
- Mount Allison University was established in 1839.
- St. Thomas University became a degree-granting school in 1934. It moved to Fredericton in 1964.
- The University of Moncton was created in 1964.

Source: Government of New Brunswick; University of New Brunswick.

NUMBER OF UNDERGRADUATE UNIVERSITY STUDENTS IN NEW BRUNSWICK

1920 4,87
1950 2,020
2005 24,808

Source: Statistics Canada

Did you know...

that Fredericton High School, established in 1785, is the oldest English language high school in Canada?

THE WORLD'S BEST CANOES

New Brunswick has some of the world's best rivers, the stately Saint John and the mighty Miramichi to name just two. Travelling these

Railway

Take a look at the map of New Brunswick. You'll see place names like Dalhousie Junction, Harvey Station and McManus Siding, and count-less others, illustrate the importance of the railway to the province.

In 1836, the provincial legislature incorporated the St. Andrews and Quebec Rail Road Company to build a rail line from St. Andrews to Lower Canada. Soon after that rail lines popped up all over. So important was rail transport that one of the conditions of Confederation was the construction of a rail line that would cross through New Brunswick, linking Halifax with Quebec.

Railways were also economically significant. In 1870 industrialist Alexander Gibson received a provincial charter to establish the New Brunswick Land and Railway Company (renamed the New Brunswick Railway Company in 1881) to transport timber from his woodlot holdings to his famous Marysville mill.

National railways got in on the action too. In 1890, Canadian Pacific was given a 999-year lease on the New Brunswick railway, and Saint John became the company's east coast port when Montreal froze over in the winter. In 1919, the Canadian National Railway was created and controlled the Grand Trunk railway that linked Moncton and Halifax. Moncton, home to a locomotive repair shop, became the heart of the CNR's Maritime activity.

In the late 1980s, though, things started to sour for the province's train business. In 1988, CN closed its repair shop in Moncton and in 1994 the CPR stopped serving regions east of Montreal. CPR tracks have been ripped up, replaced by walking trails. Today, CN carries goods and passengers from Saint John and Moncton to Levi, Quebec along the province's north shore. In 2004, there were 1,794 km of track in the province.

river highways for business and pleasure has long been part of New Brunswick life and its not surprising that the province was home to the Chestnut Canoe Company, a world-renowned canoe manufacturer.

Started by Fredericton's Chestnut family in the late 19th century, the company built its first canoe in 1897. Drawing on Maliseet craftsmanship, the company patented its wood-canvas canoe in 1905, selling them for $35. The company expanded several times, even surviving a major fire in 1921 that destroyed the main production site.

In 1974, the company opened a huge factory in Oromocto., but facing difficult times, the company folded, building its last canoe in 1979. Over the course of its illustrious history, more than 100,000 Chestnut canoes were sold to its biggest retailer, the Hudson's Bay Company.

DUNGARVON WHOOPER

One of the province's best-known trains was the *Dungarvon Whooper* (pronounced "hooper"), a passenger train that ran from Newcastle to Fredericton. The train got its name from a spooky story of the paranormal. Legend has it that a young lumber camp cook was violently murdered along the Dungarvan River, a tributary of the Miramichi. After his death, the wails, or 'whoops', of the victim's ghost were said to ring out in the woods on still nights. The train's horn reminded residents of the spooky sound.

GETTING AROUND

Just a century ago, New Brunswickers traveled their province by horse-drawn carriage, train and boat. As it did elsewhere, the introduction of the automobile revolutionized the way New Brunswickers traveled.

Did you know...

that Sussex Corner baker Walter Donelly invented the ice cream cone? Maybe this isn't surprising. After all, nearby Sussex is Canada's dairy capital.

- On January 31, 1851, Saint Johners are introduced to Audromonon Carriage, the first 'horseless carriage' in New Brunswick.
- In May 1901, Alex Carter and Walter S. Bowness build New Brunswick's first automobile in their Moncton shop.
- On a September day in 1902, J.C. Miller of Millerton makes the province's first long distance car trip. In 11 bumpy hours he travels from Newcastle to Fredericton.
- On May 5, 1905, Walter Holley of Saint John is granted the province's first automobile license.
- On December 1, 1922, New Brunswick drivers make the switch and start driving on the right-hand side of the road.

Source: Government of New Brunswick. Culture and Sport Secretariat.

AUTOMOBILE REGISTRATIONS

1905	12
1915	1,900
1935	31,217
1955	106,648
1975	288,658
2003	467,574

Source: Historical Statistics of Canada

Chrysler costs, May 1928		Chrysler costs in 2006	
Chrysler Sedan	$850	**Chrysler Sebring**	$25,200
Coup	$870	**Sebring Convertible**	$36,455
Roadster	$870	**Chrysler 300**	$30,655
DeLuxe Sedan	$1000	**Crossfire SRT6**	$66,630
		Roadster	

Sources: News fit to Print Autonet.ca, MRSP, June 2006

Did you know...

that Babe Ruth enjoyed of hunting in New Brunswick?

COVERED BRIDGES

Not so long ago, hundreds of covered bridges dotted the province. Today, there are 65 left, including the world's longest at Hartland. Many are in Kings County near Sussex, the covered bridge capital of Atlantic Canada.

Source: Government of New Brunswick.

ELECTRICITY

Steam-generated electricity was first produced for sale in New Brunswick by the Saint John Electric Light Company in 1884. Over the next 36 years, 20 companies provided unreliable and expensive power to New Brunswickers. The 1920 creation of the New Brunswick Electric Power Commission and NB Power brought more reliable electrification.

In the 1950s, New Brunswick went gaga for hydro-electricity. In 1955, the Beechwood hydroelectric dam was built, and in 1968 Mactaquac went online. New Brunswick entered the nuclear power age in 1983 when the Point Lepreau nuclear power station began operation. Today it contributes 25 to 30 percent of New Brunswick's power.

NO SWEETER HISTORY

World famous New Brunswick chocolatiers, the Ganong Brothers, have been concocting their sweet treats for more than a century. In 1873, James and Gilbert Ganong opened a small grocery store but soon focussed on chocolate and candy. Over the years, Ganong's has been a true family business. All four company presidents have been family members.

There have been several sweet milestones for Ganong's. In 1885, the company first produced its trademark Chicken Bones, crunchy cinnamon candy with a chocolate filling. In 1895, they introduced the first Canadian

Did you know...

that in 1973 Ron Turcotte of Grand Falls won horse racing's Triple Crown on his famous mount, Secretariat?

Did you know...

lollipop and, in 1910, the first chocolate bar. Ganong's signature Pal-o-mine chocolate bar was invented in 1920 and in 1932 the company was the first to manufacture a heart shaped box for chocolate, initially a Christmas feature but soon a Valentine's Day staple. Today, boxed chocolates, made and sold by 400 employees, are Ganong's biggest sellers.

PAINLESS PARKER

In 1872, Edgar Randolph Parker was born in the small village of Tynemouth Creek, near Saint John. In seeking fame and fortune, Parker decided to take a bite out of the Big Apple. He attended dental school and established his practice – and his reputation for eccentricity – on the streets of New York City.

Part huckster, part doctor, Parker started a travelling dental practice featuring "painless dentistry," using over-the-top publicity stunts to drum up business. He employed marching bands and tight rope walkers to hover between skyscrapers. He even removed the teeth of lions and tigers

Take 5 FIVE SWEET OFFERINGS
FROM GANONG BROTHERS

1. Chicken bones
2. Pal-o-mine chocolate bar
3. The Red Wrap, 5 pound box
4. Fruitfulls
5. Jelly Beans

Did you know...

that New Brunswick began issuing marriage licences to same-sex couples on July 4, 2005?

to the applause of a New York crowd and once claimed to have pulled 357 teeth in one day, all of which he proudly displayed in a macabre necklace.

His shtick worked. By the end of his career, his 30 offices on the U.S. west coast employed 70 and earned $3 million. He died in San Francisco, California on November 9, 1952.

WHERE THE WATER RUNS DEEP AND STILL

Legend has it that Lake Utopia, near St. George in southern New Brunswick, is home to a lake monster. Mi'kmaq legends tell of a giant serpentine creature and eyewitness reports dating to the 1800s and as recently as 1996, corroborate its existence.

Sightings have been recorded every three to five years, prompting one crypto zoologist to hypothesize that the monster is migratory, travelling out to sea through the deep channel connecting Lake Utopia and the Atlantic, and regularly returning to the lake. This same expert asserts that the creature is amphibious, capable of holding its breath for long spans of time.

Of course, not everyone is convinced. Critics charge that the small lake could not sustain such a beast. They argue that sightings of the so-called sea monster are actually eels, fish, logs or common mammals such as otters or beaver.

They Said It

"Our formulas are important, but a key factor also is the water. It comes from an under ground spring three miles out of town, and our formulas are attuned to this unique water – they don't work anywhere else."
—Whidden Ganong, on the secret to his company's candy.

that the dreaded disease leprosy once plagued New Brunswickers? Victims were abandoned to fend for themselves until a 1944 quarantine station was established for sufferers on Sheldrake Island, in the mouth of the Miramichi River.

THE PARIS CREW

In the mid 19th century Saint John rowing was very popular. Interested in the sport, Saint Johners Robert Foulton, Elijah Ross, Samuel Hutton and James Price pitched in to buy a boat. Little did they know they would row to fame and into the history books.

By 1866, the team of four were serious rowing contenders, winning every race they entered. In 1867, a huge regatta was held in Paris and, keen to send the winning rowers, the city of Saint John raised the $7,000 to fund their trip. The Saint Johners crew won and returned, like heroes, to the Port City as the 'Paris Crew'.

In 1870, the Paris Crew accepted a challenge from an English crew. In their first race, the English won and so the Paris Crew challenged them to a second, to be held on the Kennebecasis River on August 23, 1871. At mid-race, when the English crew faltered and their captain, James Renforth slumped over in his seat, the Paris crew blew past the Brits, setting a record time.

The win was soured by the sad fate of their opponents. Within hours, Renforth died. Showing proper respect, the Saint John revelry

They Said It

"I've had enough credible people, in my own lifetime, come to me and tell me their experiences that I really don't doubt that there is some creature."

—Norma Stewart, crypto zoologist, on the Sea Monster of Lake Utopia

Did you know...

> that the fountain in front of City Hall was erected in 1885. That makes "Freddie, the little nude dude," as he is affectionately known, two years older than the Statue of Liberty.

was cancelled and flags were lowered to half-mast. For years the Renforth regatta was held as a memorial to the British rower, a great challenger of the Paris Crew. In 1956, the Paris Crew was named to the Canadian Sports Hall of fame.

Weblinks

Heritage Resources, Saint John, A Celebration of Our Community
http://198.164.154.3/~Heritage/index.htm
This glimpse into Saint John's past covers a wide range of topics, including the fate of Black Loyalists who settled in that city, North America's first mental institution, and the Port City's marine heritage.

New Brunswick's Covered Bridges (and Lighthouses)
http://bridges.nblighthouses.com/
For news and information concerning New Brunswick's 65 covered bridges and 70 lighthouses, this is your site.

How well do you know New Brunswick?
http://new-brunswick.net/new-brunswick/quiz.html
Link to this website of the New Brunswick government to take this quiz about New Brunswick, then and now.

Economy

GROSS DOMESTIC PRODUCT (GDP): TOTAL VALUE OF GOODS AND SERVICES PRODUCED BY THE PROVINCE

- In 2005, New Brunswick's GDP was valued at $23,727,000,000, the 8th highest in Canada.
- Per capita GDP: $31,552 (10th in Canada)
- GDP growth in 2005: 0.5 percent
- National GDP growth rate in 2005: 2.9 percent

Source: Statistics Canada; ScotiaBank.

INCOME

- Per capita income in 2005: $26,644 (84.5 percent of Canadians' per capita income)
- Average annual family income: $64,527
- Canadian average family income $79,396

New Brunswick incomes have increased in the past five years. In 2001, New Brunswickers earned an average $661.21 a week; by 2005, this had grown to $785.21. Nationally, Canadians earned $805.57 a week in 2005, the highest wages being in the Yukon ($917.21) and lowest in Prince Edward Island, ($725.36).

RICH AND POOR

Annually, 7 percent of New Brunswickers earned less than $5,000. At the other end of the pay spectrum, 15 percent earned more than $50,000.

Sources: Source: Government of New Brunswick; Statistics Canada; Fraser Institute.

BY THE HOUR

In 2006, New Brunswickers over the age of 15 earned an average hourly salary of $15.79. Men earned an average $16.60 and women, $14.95. Unionized workers earned an average $20.75 while non-unionized earned $14.01. Minimum wage is $6.70.

Source: Statistics Canada; NB Dept. of Post-Secondary Education and Training.

EXPENDITURES

In 2004 New Brunswick households spent an average $51,531.

DEBT

Collectively New Brunswickers owe $6.734 billion.
- 60.1 percent on mortgages
- 15.1 percent on vehicle loans
- 8.2 percent on student loans
- 5.2 percent on lines of credit
- 5.2 percent on credit cards

Source: Statistics Canada.

TAXES

- Provincial sales tax: 8 percent
- Combined provincial sales tax and federal GST (HST): 14 percent
- Average income tax paid by New Brunswickers: $4,134
- Personal income tax rates: 9.68 percent to 17.84 percent
- Small business corporate tax rate: 1.5 percent

Sources: Canada Revenue Agency; NB Department of Finance.

TOP FIVE EXPENSES
OF NEW BRUNSWICK HOUSEHOLDS (2004)

1. **Income tax** ($9,431)
2. **Shelter** ($8,802)
3. **Transportation** ($7,748)
4. **Food** ($6,063)
5. **Insurance** ($3,326)

Source: Statistics Canada.

TAX FREEDOM DAY
(DATE ON WHICH EARNINGS NO LONGER GO TO TAXES, 2005)
New Brunswickers stop paying their taxes 12 days earlier than the national average. Over all, the province has the third latest tax freedom day.

Tax freedom day, nationally	June 26
Alberta	May 31
Saskatchewan	June 14
New Brunswick	June 14
Prince Edward Island	June 14
Nova Scotia	June 15

 TOP FIVE SOURCES
OF NEW BRUNSWICKERS' DEBT (VALUE)

1. **Mortgages** ($40,800)
2. **Vehicle loan** ($10,500)
3. **Student loan** ($10,100)
4. **Line of credit** ($9,800)
5. **Credit card/installment debt** ($2,400)

Source: Statistics Canada.

Newfoundland and Labrador	June 20
Ontario	June 21
Manitoba	June 22
British Columbia	June 23
Quebec	July 7

Source: The Fraser Institute

New Brunswick Ingenuity

Did you ever wonder whose idea it was to match your luggage with your ticket number so you'd (in theory) never lose it? Ever think about the person who came up with central heating, your favourite word game or a saw capable of gnawing through the toughest of trees? Clever New Brunswickers are responsible for these inventions and countless others.

- In 1839, Saint Johners James Elliott and Alexander McAvity invented something to help the world breathe a little easier – a Self-contained Underwater Breathing Apparatus, the SCUBA tank.
- In 1843, Saint John's own John E. Turnbull saved women's knuckles from the scrub board by patenting a manual clothes washer.
- In 1845, Frederictonian Benjamin F. Tibbitts got everyone steamed up with his patent on a marine compound steam engine. This changed forever the operation and speed of ships sailing the world's waters.
- In 1871, Saint John's Andrew J. Stewart revolutionized laundry. His invention of a cold-water soap paved the way for Tide and Cheer that thankfully replaced borax, ammonia, naphtha and paint thinner as clothes cleaners.
- In 1880, Thomas Campbell of Saint John turned the world on to hot- and cold-water faucets.
- In 1882, Monctonian John Mitchell Lyons permanently attached

EMPLOYMENT

Labour Force	389,600
Employed	358,500
Unemployed	31,100
Unemployment Rate	8.0 percent
Participation Rate	63.7 percent

travelers to their luggage with the Separable Baggage Check.
- In 1895, Saint Johner Philias Bertrand made life easier for woodsmen everywhere with his invention of the Inserted Saw Tooth.
- In 1900, Joseph S. Clark of St. George turned the canned meat industry upside down by patenting a key for the bottom of the can to open it anywhere, anytime.
- In 1920, Saint Johner Robert T. Mawhinney got down and dirty, patenting the dump box for the back of what would become dump trucks.
- In 1922, Rothesay's Wallace R. Turnbull patented the Variable Pitch Propeller, allowing propeller driven planes to change the speed and pitch of their propellers to better match flying conditions.
- In 1924, Sackville's L.W. Daman got people heated with the Pipeless Furnace, a central unit and a single floor drill.
- In 1926, Edward R. McDonald of Shediac patented the wildly popular and enduring board game, Scrabble.
- In 1933, Deer Island's Hartley A. Wentworth combined fish liver with chocolate in an effort to make a palatable children's vitamin.

Source: Government of New Brunswick, Culture and Sport Secretariat.

GOOD AND SERVICES

Percentage working in goods production	21.8
Service Industry	78.2

Source: Statistics Canada.

SECTORS IN WHICH NEW BRUNSWICKERS ARE EMPLOYED (PERCENTAGE OF ALL WORKERS)

Trade	16.6
Health care and social assistance	13.4
Manufacturing	10.2
Educational services	7.5
Accommodation and food services	6.3
Transportation and warehousing	6.0
Business, building, support services	6.0
Public administration	6.0
Construction	5.3
Professional, scientific, technical services	4.3
Finance, insurance, real estate and leasing	3.9
Information, culture and recreation	3.6
Forestry, fishing, mining, oil and gas	3.3
Agriculture	1.9
Utilities	0.9
Other services	4.7

Source: Statistics Canada.

PUBLIC ADMINISTRATION

Exactly 94,592 New Brunswickers work in public administration, meaning one in every eight New Brunswickers is employed by government or a government agency.

- 29.3 percent work for the provincial government
- 23.5 percent work for local governments (including school boards)
- 23.2 percent work for health and social services
- 14.6 percent work for the federal government (including military)

- 6.9 percent work for government business enterprises
- 2.4 percent work for universities

Source: Statistics Canada, NB Department of Human Resources.

GENDER GAP
- Percentage of men who work: 68.7
- Percentage of women: 58.1
- The average income of men age 15 and older in New Brunswick in 2000: $29,767
- Average income of women: $18,586 (women earn 62 percent of men's earnings)
- Percentage of men earning less than $10,000/year: 20
- Percentage of women earning less than $10,000/year: 31

Source: Statistics Canada Labour Force Survey.

SHARING THE WEALTH
In 2004, New Brunswickers donated $133,670,000 to charity. The median amount they donated was $280, fifty dollars more than the national median of $230.

Source: Statistics Canada.

HOW WE GET TO WORK
- 79.6 percent drive their own vehicles
- 9.9 percent carpool
- 7.3 percent walk
- 1.8 percent use public transportation
- 2.1 percent get to work using other means

Source: Statistics Canada.

Did you know...

that New Brunswickers spend an average $2,344 on home repairs and renovations? Nationally, Canadians homeowners spent $2,910.

HOUSING

New Brunswick has the second lowest housing costs. Only Newfoundland and Labrador has lower. New Brunswick's housing costs are just 53 percent of the national average and 37 percent of British Columbia's, the nation's highest.

Canada	$162,709
Newfoundland and Labrador	$76,283
New Brunswick	$86,538
Saskatchewan	$93,065
Manitoba	$97,670
Prince Edward Island	$100,657
Nova Scotia	$101,515
Quebec	$110,668
Alberta	$159,698
Ontario	$199,884
British Columbia	$230,645

Source: Statistics Canada.

Take 5 TOP FIVE GDP-GENERATING SERVICE SECTORS IN NEW BRUNSWICK (PERCENT OF GDP)

1. **Finance, Insurance, Real Estate, Renting, Leasing, Company Management** (15 percent)
2. **Public Administration** (9 percent)
3. **Health Care and Social Assistance** (7 percent)
4. **Retail Trade** (6 percent)
5. **Transportation and Warehousing / Educational services** (5 percent each)

Source: Statistics Canada.

GOVERNMENT DOUGH:
WHERE NEW BRUNSWICK GETS ITS CASH

Total government revenue	$6.23 billion
Percentage from equalization payments	22.9
Income taxes	20.5 percent
Sales Tax	13 percent
Royalties	1.1 percent
Canada Health Transfer	7.8 percent
Property tax	5.6 percent
Canada Social Transfer	3.4 percent
Other	25.7 percent

Source: NB Department of Finance.

TOTAL GOVERNMENT EXPENDITURE:
HOW NEW BRUNSWICK SPENDS ITS CASH

Total expenditure	$6.21 billion
Percentage spent on Health	38.7 percent
Education	19.5 percent
Debt Service	9.1 percent
Transportation	6.3 percent
Income Security and Housing	5.3 percent
Other	21.1 percent

Source: Government of New Brunswick Office of the Comptroller.

Take 5 TOP FIVE GDP-GENERATING
INDUSTRIES IN NEW BRUNSWICK
(PERCENT OF GDP)

1. **Manufacturing** (13 percent)
2. **Construction** (5 percent)
3. **Agriculture, Forestry, Fishing and Hunting** (4 percent)
4. **Utilities** (3 percent)
5. **Mining, Oil and Gas Extraction** (1 percent)

Source: Statistics Canada.

Bio LORD BEAVERBROOK

No discussion of New Brunswickers with business and political acumen is complete without mention of William Maxwell Aitken, known formally as Lord Beaverbrook. From humble beginnings as the son of a Presbyterian minister in rural New Brunswick, Aitken went on to become a savvy business tycoon who was not only a millionaire before his 30th birthday, but also a friend to world leaders (including Sir Winston Churchill and Canadian Prime Minister, R.B. Bennett), a political tour de force and head of a newspaper empire. Add to this his penchant for philanthropy, and it is little wonder that this New Brunswicker has left a lasting legacy in his home province.

Young Aitken was not interested in following in his father's footsteps. Instead, at age 24, Aitken sharpened his business acumen by joining a company whose main objective was to buy small companies and turn them into profit-making machines. Before long he earned his first million. He then struck out on his own, heading to Montreal where he scooped up companies on the verge of bankruptcy and applied to them his midas touch.

Aitken was also a political animal. He crossed the pond to become a Conservative Member of Parliament and Canada's military representative in Britain during WWI. His loyalty to the Crown earned him a knighthood and the handle "Lord Beaverbrook." At war's end he left the civil service to devote himself to his newspaper business and writing.

Beaverbrook's legacy is not without controversy. Recently, a "hullabalo" attached to his name has plagued Fredericton's Beaverbrook Art Gallery. Shortly before his death, Beaverbrook established the gallery, reportedly instructing the Canadian and UK Beaverbrook Foundations to fill the institution with paintings and artwork of his personal collection, including priceless pieces by Dali, the Group of Seven and Emily Carr.

A dispute erupted in 2003, however, as Beaverbrook heirs laid claim to the pieces, which they wish to sell to raise money for the Beaverbrook foundation. The gallery, meanwhile, maintains its right to hold the pieces indefinitely. The issue has been turned to arbitration.

GOVERNMENT DEBT
- Total debt $6.836 billion (2005 figure)
- Annual interest $359.3 million
- Debt as a percentage of GDP   29.3

INFLATION
- In 2005, inflation stood at 2.4 percent.
- The national rate of inflation in 2005: 2.0 percent

Source: 2005 figure: NB Dept of Finance; Statistics Canada.

BUSINESS
New Brunswick has a total of 42,244 businesses. A whopping 97 percent of these are "small," with fewer than 50 employees.
- 42.6 percent have no payroll employees
- 33.5 percent have fewer than five employees
- 16.6 percent have 5-19 employees
- 4.7 percent have 20-49 employees
- 2.5 percent have 50-499 employees
- 0.1 percent have 500 or more employees

A third of New Brunswickers work for a small business; 19 percent work for a company with 50-499 of employees and 48 percent for companies with more than 500 employees.

In 2004, 207 businesses went bankrupt.

Source: Government of New Brunswick. Canadian Federation of Independent Business.

EXPORTS
In 2005, exports were worth $10.7 billion and accounted for 45 percent of New Brunswick's GDP and 2.6 percent of Canada's total exports.

Source: Government of New Brunswick, Department of Finance.

ENERGY

Energy exports bring in over half of the province's total export revenue. Petroleum is worth a cool $5.8 billion and electricity $226 million. Saint John is home to Canada's largest oil refinery. This facility alone reaped $5.8 billion in export dollars in 2005. New Brunswick's power generating prowess is also impressive. The province generates 4,200 MW3 of power – by comparison, Nova Scotia generates 2,300 MW and Prince Edward Island just 200 MW.

Sources: Government of New Brunswick, Department of Finance; Atlantic Center for Energy.

Take 5 BUZZ HARGROVE'S FIVE TOP WORDS TO DESCRIBE NEW BRUNSWICKERS

Buzz Hargrove, president of The Canadian Auto Workers Union, is one of Canada's most powerful labour leaders. Born Basil Eldon Hargrove in Bath, New Brunswick, he was the sixth of 10 children. Hargrove overcame both poverty and the fact that he did not finish highschool. He found a job on the line of a Windsor, Ontario Chrysler plant and eventually emerged as a fiery national labour leader, a man whose power rivals that of the country's business elite. Hargrove says he travels home often and enjoys spending time with fellow New Brunswickers. Hargrove shares with us what he thinks are the five best words to describe New Brunswickers.

1. Socialist: I have traveled the country and the world. I think New Brunswickers have sense of community and support for one another and really treat everyone as equals. They really do believe everyone should be treated on an equal basis. I came from a broken family and when I was growing up I lived with a guy for a few years who didn't charge me a nickel. He wasn't working and when he worked, he only worked a couple of days. He was a conservative and he voted conservative but he was a socialist. Every kid that came along and need-

Did you know...

that 51 percent of all New Brunswick exports are produced by companies with fewer than 50 employees?

DIGGIN' IT

Second to New Brunswick's wealth of forest resources is its impressive mineral wealth. For its size, the province contributes a great deal to the

ed a place to stay he always found a bed for them and a room to stay. He didn't make a lot of money but he always found a way to put food on the table. That's the sense of community that I see in New Brunswick and I see it still when I go home.

2. Fun-loving: Fun loving because they love to party. Boy, when I go down home everybody wants to get together, get the guitars, get the fiddles, and have a few beers and a few laughs. They work hard but they always find time to play.

3. Hard-working: Wherever I go, employers love to hire people from New Brunswick. New Brunswickers are really viewed as hard-working people.

4. Conciliatory: I know a lot of people from New Brunswick. People like Frank McKenna, for example, and a number of other people I meet as head of the (Canadian Auto Workers) union in different situations are always trying to find a way to work with the broader community. They are very conciliatory to one another and open to the point of views of others.

5. Determined: I've always been impressed by the determination of so many New Brunswickers I've met.

The Irving Empire

An industrial empire started by Kenneth Colin ("KC") Irving continues to have controlling interests in nearly every major New Brunswick industry. The Irving company had its start rather innocently. In 1924, a young KC worked as a gas station manager with Imperial Oil. When he reportedly had an argument with company officials, he simply borrowed money to start his own oil company. The rest, as they say, is history.

KC's business expanded quickly to include service stations and garages. By the 1930s, he was acquiring bussing and trucking companies that owed him money. His industrial spirit pushed him to manufacture his own fleet of trucks and purchase ships to transport his oil around the world.

With the death of his father in the early 1930s, KC inherited an established lumber business. From there, Irving purchased the New Brunswick Railway Company, less for the tracks, than the timber-rich tracts of land on which they laid. With this land base, Irving started Irving Pulp and Paper.

Although the Irving's massive undertakings have contributed much to the New Brunswick economy, he has had his fair share of critics. Irving's hold on the media has often been condemned as being a self-serving impediment to a free press. Meanwhile, his company has been accused of sundering the province's resources and environment for private gain. Then there are criticisms of the tax shelters that have shielded Irving wealth from the taxman. Regardless of how New Brunswickers feel about Irving and company, he has gone down in history as one of the most influential industrialists New Brunswick, Canada, and even North America has ever produced. When KC Irving died in 1992, his sons James K. Irving, Arthur L. Irving, and John E. Irving carried on the family business.

Take 5 **FIVE SECTORS WITH THE MOST BUSINESSES (PERCENTAGE OF ALL BUSINESSES IN THE PROVINCE).**

1. **Retail trade** (4,950, 11.7 percent)
2. **Construction** (4,844, 11.5 percent)
3. **Agriculture, forestry, fishing and hunting** (4,839, 11.5 percent)
4. **Professional, scientific and technical** (3,244, 7.7 percent)
5. **Transportation and warehousing** (2,898, 6.9 percent)

Source: Canada/New Brunswick Business Service Centre.

country's overall mineral industry. It ranks first in Canada for lead, zinc, bismuth and antimony production, second for peat production, and third for silver.

The bulk of New Brunswick's mineral riches consist of base metals in the north, potash in the south, coal around Grand Lake, and gold in the central areas. In 2005, $12.1 million was spent on mineral exploration in New Brunswick, up 1.1 percent over the year before and representing a considerable increase over the $3.2 million spent in 2002. The industry supports the employment of more than 3,000 people and injects $700 million into provincial coffers annually.

Take 5 **TOP FIVE EXPORTS (VALUE)**

1. **Energy** ($6.2 billion)
2. **Forestry products** ($1.8 billion)
3. **Agriculture and fishing** ($1.3 billion)
4. **Industrial goods and materials** ($801 million)
5. **Machinery and equipment** ($459 million)

Source: Government of New Brunswick, Department of Finance.

Fries with that?

In January 1957, the first McCain french fry plant opened in Florenceville, New Brunswick. That first year, 30 employees produced goods generating $152,678 in sales. Fast-forward to 2004 when McCain Foods Limited boasted 20,000 employees, 55 production facilities in a dozen countries, and sales of $5.8 billion. The business genius behind this phenomenally successful food company is a New Brunswick family from rural Carleton County.

In 1927, Harrison McCain was born to a well-to-do Florenceville potato farmer. In the 1950s, Harrison and his younger brother, Wallace, used their inheritance to start the first frozen fry operation in eastern Canada. McCain's has gone on to diversify. Globally the company produces a range of food products, including other potato products, frozen vegetables, frozen pizzas, fruit juices, cakes and pies.

In recent years the phenomenal success of McCain Foods Limited was eclipsed by news of a McCain family feud. In 1993, brother Wallace was shut out of the family business. All was not lost for Wallace, however as he and his sons have turned Maple Leaf Foods into yet another food empire.

McCain Foods, continued under Harrison's watch, expanded and become a global leader among food processors. In 1992, Harrison's achievements were recognized when he was named a Companion of the Order of Canada. In 2003, Forbes magazine named Harrison one of the world's richest men, pegging the then 75 year old's wealth at $1.5 billion, making him one of Canada's 14 billionaires that year.

Sadly, just a year later, Harrison McCain lost his long battle with kidney disease. His nephew, Allison, assumed the helm of the family business, which is still based out of picturesque Florenceville, in the heart of New Brunswick's rich potato belt.

Did you know...

that spruce is New Brunswick's dominant tree species?

FOREST INDUSTRY

The woods have long been a pillar of New Brunswick's economy. Cut off from her Baltic lumber source by a French blockade, Britain turned to British North America for much-needed lumber. New Brunswick's fine stands and rivers well-placed to transport felled logs guaranteed the rise of New Brunswick's timber industry.

New Brunswick has 5.9 million acres of productive forest land. Annually, the forestry industry is worth $2.1 billion. In 2001, New Brunswick was home to 69 forest-reliant communities, the highest concentration of such communities in Canada.

Approximately 23,400 New Brunswickers – 1 in 11 workers – are directly and indirectly employed in forestry. Collectively they bring home annual wages of more than $1.1 billion. In recent years, mill closures, the result of decreased world demand for paper products, has resulted in the industry faltering somewhat. In 2005-2006, forest product exports fell by 22 percent, and only a modest improvement is anticipated in the near future.

They Said It

"This industry has been a blessing for us, no doubt about it."
— **Stan Smith, Mayor of St. George's NB, on fish farming**

Did you know...

that DDT (dichloro-diphenyl-trichloro-ethane) was sprayed on New Brunswick forests to combat Spruce Budworm for the first time in 1952? Proven to be harmful to wildlife and human health, use of DDT was discontinued in 1968.

FORESTRY FACTS

- Value of forest product exports in 2005: $1.8 billion
- Percentage from paper: 34
- From lumber: 29 percent
- From wood pulp: 17 percent
- Percentage of New Brunswick woodland that is crown land: 51
- Percentage owned privately: 29
- Percentage that is industrial freehold: 18
- The province's 7 pulp and paper mills produce 2.5 million tonnes of product a year.
- 65 mills generate 950 million board feet/year.

Source: Government of New Brunswick; Natural Resources Canada.

Did you know...

that nearly 4.2 million kg of wild blueberries, worth approximately $7 million dollars, are harvested each year in New Brunswick? This represents 16 percent of wild blueberries harvested in Canada.

Take 5 — TOP FIVE FISH EXPORTS
(VALUE, 2004)

1. **Lobster**, $388.8 million
2. **Salmon**, $158 million
3. **Crab**, $130.6 million
4. **Herring**, $40.6 million
5. **Sardine**, $19.3 million

Source: Government of New Brunswick.

FISH

In 2004, 101,000 tonnes of fish and seafood products were exported, reeling in $824 million for New Brunswick. The fishery has nearly 3,000 commercial vessels, 137 processing plants, employs more than 12,000 people and is worth nearly $200 million in annual landings. In all, 20 New Brunswick communities rely on the fishing industry.

Source: Government of New Brunswick.

FISH FARMING

New Brunswick is following in the footsteps of Scandinavian countries as it establishes a lucrative fish farming industry. In 2005, New Brunswick aquaculture was worth $181 million (twice the value of potatoes) and accounted for 34 percent of all aquaculture production in Canada – only BC has a larger aquaculture industry.

Although New Brunswick fish farms produce a number of species

Did you know...

that beer exports brought in $38.7 million in 2004? When it comes to exported food commodities, beer was second only to potatoes.

Take 5 TOP FIVE COUNTRIES
THAT BUY NEW BRUNSWICK SEAFOOD (2004)

1. **United States**
2. **Japan**
3. **Dominican Republic**
4. **Denmark**
5. **China**

Source: Government of New Brunswick.

including trout, oysters and mussels, salmon is by far the most important species and has been since 1979 when New Brunswickers first farmed the species.

In 2004, 99 salmon farming sites produced salmon for export valued at $158 million. Almost 1,300 New Brunswickers worked at salmon farms, and another 560 processed the fish. Although undeniably lucrative, fish farming has its critics. They charge that overcrowded fish farms cause disease that put wild species at risk and generate pollution.

Sources: Government of New Brunswick; Statistics Canada; Conservation Council.

AGRICULTURE

Just 2 percent of New Brunswick land is used for agricultural purposes, but from this the province reaps a hefty reward. In 2005, 3,000 farms pulled in more than $425 million in total cash receipts, equaling nearly $15 million in total net income. In 2004, over 8,200 New Brunswickers worked on farms. New Brunswick's three most productive agricultural regions are in Carleton, Madawaska and Kings Counties; together they account for 50 percent of New Brunswick's farm income.

Source: New Brunswick Department of Agriculture, Fisheries and Aquaculture; Statistics Canada.

POTATO PARTICULARS

More than 50 varieties of potatoes are grown in New Brunswick on more than 26,600 hectares. New Brunswick grows 14.5 percent of Canada's potatoes; they are sold in more than 20 nations.

Sources: Potatoes New Brunswick; Government of New Brunswick.

Take 5 TOP FIVE DESTINATION OF EXPORTED AGRI-FOODS (VALUE, 2004)

1. **United States** — $293.2 million
2. **Venezuela** — $12.8 million
3. **Japan** — $4.5 million
4. **China** — $2.2 million
5. **Korea/Philippines** — $0.1 million

Source: Government of New Brunswick.

TRANSPORTATION INFRASTRUCTURE

- Airports: 26
- Number with paved runways: 16
- Number of major airports: 3 (Saint John, Fredericton and Moncton)
- Kilometres of road: 18,000
- Length of the TransCanada: 523 km
- Length of railway tracks: 1,275 km
- Ports: 5 (Saint John, Belldune, Bayside Port Corporation, Dalhousie, Miramichi)

Sources: Tourism New Brunswick; TransCanada Highway; Government of New Brunswick.

SELLING THE "PICTURE PROVINCE"

In 2003, tourism generated $1.1 billion and $272 million in tax revenue. In all, 1.86 million people visited the province; 31 percent were from the Maritimes, 24 percent from the US, 23 percent from Ontario and 18 percent from Quebec.

Source: Government of New Brunswick.

They Said It

"I've invested a lot of faith in this car and I'm very, very happy."
— **New Brunswick Premier Richard Hatfield, in 1974, at which time he had sunk $5 million into Malcom Bricklin's dodgy car**

Did you know...

that in 2005 the chickens of New Brunswick clucked their way through the delivery of more than 15 million eggs? The value of the hens' contribution: $28 million.

THE BRICKLIN BUNGLE

One of the lasting legacies of Richard Hatfield's premiership was his commitment to diversifying the province's economy. In the 1970s, Hatfield teamed up with young upstart, Malcolm Bricklin, to manufacture a New Brunswick-made sports car. This collaboration demonstrated Hatfield's optimism for New Brunswick's economic future. "We are not just building a car, we're building a better New Brunswick," Hatfield said.

In 1972, Hatfield's government announced its backing of young Bricklin's venture and in 1974 a Saint John Bricklin factory opened to much fanfare. Just two years later the Bricklin venture was bankrupt. Only 2,854 of the vehicles, which retailed for $6,000, had been built and taxpayers were on the hook for $23 million.

Why did the Bricklin dream become the Bricklin bungle? Much of the blame rests with the car's poor design. Promoted as a car rich in safety features, it was appallingly poor in design features. The car's hydraulic

Take 5 THE FIVE OFFICIAL
FACTORY COLOURS OF BRICKLINS

1. **Safety Red**
2. **Safety Orange**
3. **Safety Green**
4. **Safety Suntan**
5. **Safety White**

gull wing doors were notorious for malfunctioning, as were its pop-up headlights. Windows and windshields leaked and, in keeping with it's "safety" theme, Bricklins inconveniently had no cigarette lighters or ashtrays. No spare tire, meant more trunk space, but it also caused a huge problem in the event of a flat. To top it off, body paint chipped and faded.

Take 5 — DEREK OLAND'S FIVE MOST INTERESTING BUSINESS STORIES.

Derek Oland, Chairman and CEO of Saint John-based Moosehead Breweries Limited, is a much admired and respected business leader. Oland has taken a family brewery to a new business level. Moosehead, one of the best-known breweries in North America, has continued to expand and evolve. Moosehead beer is now distributed in 15 countries. Oland has done much for his province – he contributes frequently to various provincial causes and has helped keep the tradition of family brewing alive. Two of his sons, Andrew and Patrick, have become the 6th Oland generation to work in the family business. Oland shares with us his thoughts on the five most interesting New Brunswick business stories.

1. **The Irving family:** I think the phenomenon of the Irving family is pretty significant. They have done an awful lot for the province, and, of course, the province has in return been good to them.
2. **The McCain family:** They have done very, very well and fortunately have remained in New Brunswick.
3. **New Brunswick's emerging entrepreneurs:** There are good stories and very bright people.
4. **David Ganong and Ganong Bros. Limited.**
5. **Moosehead:** Moosehead would be another success story. I feel very good about it. I've always said I wanted to hand the company off the next generation in better shape. I wasn't always sure that I could but now I am.

Weblinks

The Bricklin
http://www.saintjohn.nbcc.nb.ca/Heritage/bricklin/index.htm
This privately constructed and maintained website tells you everything you want to know (and some things you don't) about New Brunswick's famous foray into the world of sports cars. Check out those groovy shirts!

Business New Brunswick Homepage
http://www.gnb.ca/0398/index-e.asp
This website, maintained by the provincial government, offers insight into all facets of the NB business world, from buying to investing.

New Brunswick Forest Products Association
http://www.nbforestry.com/
This website tells you all about New Brunswick's most important industry, the forest industry. This multifaceted website offers you the latest forestry news and statistics and has a "School House" section full of ideas for teaching kids about this important industry.

Culture

New Brunswick has a rich and varied cultural life. It has been built upon the diverse ancestry of the First People, newcomers such as the French, English and Scots, and other nationalities who have more recently made the province their home. The culture of the province has been shaped by the land, sea, forests and communities that make up the Picture Province.

MOVIE BUSINESS

- Number of movie theatres in New Brunswick: 12
- Number of paid admissions to movies in theatres in 2004-5: 1.73 million
- Average spending of New Brunswick households in movie theatres in 2003: $72
- Number of drive-in theatres in New Brunswick: 5
- Number of paid admissions to movies in drive-ins in 2004-55: 43,000
- Annual per-capita attendance at theatres and drive-ins in New Brunswick in 2004-5: 2.3
- Annual per-capita attendance at theatres and drive-ins in Canada in 2004-5: 3.8

Source: Statistics Canada.

that New Brunswickers spend an average of 23.7 hours a week watching TV? Women over age 18 watch most – 28.4 hours a week.

FILM MAKING

New Brunswick has a vibrant film-making community. A film-making co-op has been in operation for 26 years and 2005 marked the province's fifth annual film festival. Originally called *Tidal Wave Film Festival*, and now renamed the *Silver Wave Film Festival*, this annual event provides a forum for filmmakers and film lovers to see great movies and further hone their craft.

Take 5 FIVE TV/FILM PERSONALITIES
FROM NEW BRUNSWICK

1. **Donald Sutherland**, actor. Hailing from Saint John, he's appeared in many Hollywood films.
2. **Robb Wells**, actor. Originally from Moncton, he is best known for his role as Ricky on the Trailer Park Boys.
3. **Harry Saltzman**, producer. Born in Saint John, he is co-creator and co-producer of the early James Bond films.
4. **Louis B. Mayer**, studio mogul. Although he was born in Russia, he was raised in Saint John, a city to which he returned several times and of which he spoke fondly. In 1924, he founded Metro-Goldwyn-Mayer (MGM) Studios.
5. **Walter Pidgeon**, actor. Born in Saint John in 1898, Pidgeon's acting career spanned from the 1930s through to the 1970s. He appeared in countless TV and movie productions and was given a star on the Hollywood Walk of Fame. He died in 1984.

DONALD SUTHERLAND

Born in Saint John in 1935, Donald Sutherland was raised a Maritimer as he grew up in Bridgewater, Nova Scotia. By age 14, he had already found his way into the entertainment business as a radio DJ.

As he was doing a stint studying engineering at the University of Toronto, he also nurtured his entertaining passion, taking part in campus productions. Soon acting became his life and he moved to London where he performed in British repertory theatre and television. He received his big break in 1970 playing Capt. Benjamin Franklin "Hawkeye" Pierce in Robert Altman's film, M*A*S*H, a role that made him a star.

After M*A*S*H other films followed, including Klute with Jane Fonda in 1971, The Day of the Locust and 1900, both in 1975. Sutherland's acting longevity is the result of his willingness to showcase his varied talents by accepting many different, challenging roles. In each movie, Sutherland's trademark is that he makes his characters "real people." The Canadian acting community has recognized Sutherland's talent, and in 2000 he received a Governor-General's Performing Arts Award and a place on Canada's Walk of Fame.

They Said It

"My knees were shaking. I was so scared I wasn't sure my voice would come out at all, but it must have been all right. I remember the applause to this day. It is probably my most wonderful memory of the city in which I was born. You can forget all the boos and cat-calls in your life but you never forget the applause."

— **Walter Pidgeon recalling his stage debut at Saint John's Imperial Theatre in 1910**

RECOGNITION FOR THE ARTS

In 2005, the Canada Council of the Arts awarded $1.9 million in grants to artists and cultural organizations in New Brunswick, up from $1.8 million between the years 2000 and 2003. In addition, $140,000 was given to 310 authors through the Public Lending Rights Program, bringing the total funding to over $2 million.

Of the other recipients, 23 artists scooped up just over $200,000 of the cash, while nearly $1.7 million was shared by 53 arts organizations. The recipients dabble in all disciplines, including arts, music, media arts, theatre, visual arts and writing and publishing. Theatre received the lion's share of just under $500,000, while visual arts came in second with $462,000. Writing and publishing took third spot with a respectable $459,000 take.

Most funding, 33 percent to be exact, went to Fredericton-based artists and organizations, while 29 percent went to Moncton. Sackville and Caraquet, and 19 other communities split the remainder. The Council once again distributed funding fairly across the board; 1.7 percent of the applications it received in 2005 came from New Brunswick and 1.6 percent of what it gave out ended up there.

Source: Canada Council.

THAT'S AN ORDER

- New Brunswick recipients of the Order of Canada: 152
- Members of the order: 105
- Officers of the order: 36
- Companions of the order: 11

Sources: Gorvernor General's Office.

Did you know...

that New Brunswickers spent more than $240 million on home entertainment in 2001? In comparison, they spent just $18 million on movie admissions and $27 million on art works and art events.

Bio DAVID ADAMS RICHARDS

Born in Newcastle on October 17, 1950, David Adams Richards is one of New Brunswick's greatest literary exports. For more than thirty years, Richards' short stories, poems, novels and plays have conveyed to readers images of his beloved Miramichi, where he spent the better part of his life before moving to Toronto.

Richards was published as a poet in the early 1970s, before writing his first novel a few years later. The Coming of Winter (1974) gave the nation its first peek at this rising literary star. Richards followed that work with Blood Ties two years later and a collection of short stories (Dancers at Night) two years after that. In 1980, he published Lives of Short Duration, the novel that many say is his best work.

The 1980s saw more Richards works. His Road to the Stilt House was followed by a trilogy of novels, the first of which, Nights Below Station Street, won him the Governor General's Award in 1988. Mercy Among the Children won him critical acclaim and helped him share with Michael Ondaatje the 2000 Scotiabank Giller prize. This is the first and only time to date that the prize has been awarded to two authors.

The book was also shortlisted for several prestigious awards, including the Pearson Canada Readers' Choice Award, the Governor General's Award, the Trillium Award, and the Thomas Raddall Atlantic Fiction Prize. The novel also won the CBA Libris award for Novel of the Year and earned Richards Author of the Year prize.

Richards has been called "one of the exceptional writers of our time" by fellow Canadian author Alistair Macleod, and the Vancouver Sun suggested he is "perhaps the greatest Canadian writer alive." Richards has said that his work, which is almost set in his home province, is "a great defense of the people I grew up with."

LIVE THEATRE

- Number of theatre companies in New Brunswick: 4
- The number of theatre performances produced in 2002-3: 631
- Number of New Brunswickers who attended live theatre in 2002-3 141,099
- Revenue generated from these performances: $2.45 million

Bio ANTONINE MAILLET

Some call her the soul of contemporary literature; others say she's created an Acadian literary tradition. But if you asked Antonine Maillet, she'd say her work avenges the wrongs done to her ancestors.

Born in 1929 in Bouctouche, the heart of Acadia, she wrote her first novel in 1958 and has since published 30 more. Her work is rooted in the history, geography and traditions of Acadia. Her novels, which are often reworked for theatre, offer an epic image of Acadia.

Unlike Acadian writers who focus on the Acadians' past, Maillet celebrates their future. She does not dwell on the 1755 expulsion but rather follows the Acadian return. The spirit of Acadia is embodied in her protagonists who tend to be illiterate, courageous women. Using the French language of 17th and 18th century Acadia, Maillet shows both Acadian suffering and their enduring strength and sense of humour.

La Sagouine, written in 1971 and translated in 1979, is perhaps Maillet's best-known book, and was at the heart of the Acadian renaissance of the 1960s and 1970s. Pelagie-la-Charrette won her the Prix Goncourt, and earned her fame in France where more than one million copies were sold.

Another work, Madam Perfecta, was a finalist for the 2002 Prix Odysse. She has been named a Companion of the Order of Canada and an Officier des Arts et des Lettres de France.

- Average spent per New Brunswick household on the performing arts in 2003: $49

Source: Statistics Canada.

LITERATURE

- Number of New Brunswick authors nominated for the Governor General's Award: 15
- Number who have won the award: 4
- Number of New Brunswick authors nominated for the Scotiabank Giller Prize: 2
- Number who have won the Scotiabank Giller Prize: 1

AND THE WINNER IS . . . WINNERS OF THE GOVERNOR GENERAL'S AWARD

- Serge Patrice Thibodeau (Moncton), *Le Quatuor de l'errance*, 1996
- Hermenegilde Chiasson (Grand-Barachois), *Conversations*, 1999
- Lynn Davies (McLeod Hill), *The Bridge that Carries the Road*, 1999
- Anne Compton (Saint John), *Processional*, 2005

Sources: Scotiabank Giller Prize; Canada Council.

Did you know...

that the New Brunswick Museum in Saint John is Canada's oldest? The institution opened its doors in 1842.

They Said It

"Acadia needs to say what it is: that it is part of Canada, that it is part of America, that it is part of the international fraternity of Francophone nations, and that it therefore has its own place in the world—a place that is unique, just as each of the world's peoples is unique."

— Antonine Maillet, at the Acadian World Congress

Did you know...

ARTS SPENDING

- Average annual spending on the Arts in New Brunswick: $595 per capita
- Average annual spending on the Arts in Canada: $720 per capita

Source: Canada Council.

ARTISTS

- Number of artists in Canada: 131,000
- Number in New Brunswick: 1,800, representing 0.46 percent of the population
- Number of museums in New Brunswick: 56
- Number of art galleries in New Brunswick: 24

Source: Source: Canada Council; Statistics Canada.

Did you know...

Take 5 — TOP FIVE ITEMS

NEW BRUNSWICKERS SPEND THEIR CULTURE DOLLARS ON

1. **Home entertainment** (56 percent)
2. **Reading** (21 percent)
3. **Photographic equipment and services** (8 percent)
4. **Art works and events** (6 percent)
5. **Movie theatre admissions/art supplies and musical instruments** (4 percent each)

Source: Canada Council.

MUSIC INDUSTRY

- Total value of the music industry on the economy: $33.3-$39.2 million
- Number of musicians in New Brunswick: 835
- Number of songwriters in New Brunswick: 265
- Industry Revenues for provincial musicians: $10.4 million
- Industry Revenues for provincial songwriters: $2.3 million
- Number of symphonies in New Brunswick: 1

Source: Music Industry Association of New Brunswick.

Take 5 — TOP FIVE MUSIC FESTIVALS

1. **Harvest Jazz and Blues Festival**
2. **La Foire Brayonne**
3. **Le Festival Acadien de Caraquet**
4. **MNB Week**
5. **La Francofete en Acadie**

Source: Music New Brunswick Inc.

Take 5 ERIC LEWIS' TOP FIVE
UP-AND-COMING MUSICAL
ACTS IN NEW BRUNSWICK.

Eric Lewis is a reporter and music reviewer for Moncton's Times & Transcript. *While he writes on a variety of topics, his preferred topic is anything and everything to do with music in New Brunswick. "There are so many it's really difficult to choose without feeling like you're leaving several acts out. But these five stand out as musicians who are just starting to really see their hard work pay off, and those who are just on the cusp of that."*

1. **Darcy Mazerolle:** Country singer from Miramichi who has been turning heads everywhere he's played in the last few years. Darcy is one of five local acts opening for Alan Jackson and Brooks & Dunn this August.

2. **Matt Anderson:** A blues guitarist from Perth Andover who doesn't need a backing band to make an impact. His phenomenal guitar skills and stage presence got him a standing ovation at the 2005 East Coast Music Awards, and he's been on people's radar ever since.

3. **The Divorcees:** A Moncton country act made up of several local music veterans who are promising to bring the long-forgotten outlaw back to country music. An album is expected later this year along with a national tour.

4. **Tracy Starr:** A Moncton rock band that has been creating a buzz for itself even though it's hardly played a show over the last few years. The band's debut album is about to explode on to the scene. The band's contemporary hard rock sound led them to a deal with U.S. record label Perris Records.

5. **Sproll:** Moncton band whose sound is transplanted from England. Capturing the popular Brit-rock sound, they've made it their own. I suspect their name will be big on a national level in the not-too-distant future.

DR. STOMPIN' TOM CONNORS

Stompin' Tom is one of the most recognized personalities to traverse the Canadian cultural landscape over the last forty years. Did you know he's a New Brunswicker? Tom Connors was born in Saint John in1936.

As a young boy he was removed from the care of his grandmother and adopted by a family from Prince Edward Island, where he spent his formative years. As a 15-year-old high school drop out, Connors set out on a 13-year hitchhiking odyssey across Canada.

A struggling artist, Connors worked a series of odd jobs to supplement his performances. Going from bar to bar, he learned to play over rowdy crowds. So loud were some gigs, that Connors learned to stomp his foot to maintain a rhythm over the din. Sometimes he stomped so hard, he damaged the stage and after a few complaints he began to carry his own stomping wood, and Stompin' Tom was born.

He got his first professional gig in 1964 at a hotel in Timmins, Ontario, a gig he kept for the next 14 months. During that time, his songs made it to the air waves and to the ears of fans around the country.

He recorded his first single, 'Carolyne', in 1965. Five years later he recorded one of his many signature songs, 'Bud the Spud'. By 1978, Connors had an arsenal of 500 songs, many of which reflected Connors' intense patriotism and his support of the "common man," particularly struggling Canadian artists.

His commitment to these ideals caused controversy in the late-1970s when Connors returned the Juno awards he'd received between

Did you know...

that Canada's first published author was from New Brunswick? Julia Hart published *St. Ursula's Convent, The Nun of Canada* in 1824.

1970 and 1975 to protest Juno awards being given to Canadians abroad. He felt that Canadians in Canada should be the ones recognized by the award and given preference on Canadian radio. He made his point with a year long media boycott.

In 1996, Connors became an Officer of the Order of Canada. The East Coast Music Association created the 'Stompin' Tom' award to honour Atlantic Canadian musicians, and he became a doctor when St. Thomas University conferred upon him an honorary Doctorate of Laws. Not bad for a high school dropout with modest New Brunswick beginnings.

DINING

- Number of restaurants, bars and caterers in the province: 1,430
- Number of people employed in the restaurant industry: 23,200
- Industry sales in 2005: $885 million
- Industry's share of provincial GDP: 4.0 percent

Source: Canadian Restaurant and Foodservices Association.

Take 5 TOP FIVE 'BIG THINGS' IN NEW BRUNSWICK:

1. **Axe in Nackawic:** 15.0 m
2. **Shediac Lobster:** 10.7 m
3. **Lumberjack in Kedgwick:** 7.6 m
4. **Fiddleheads at Plaster Rock:** 7.3 m
5. **Atlantic Salmon** (Restigouche Sam) in Campbellton: 6.6 m

Source: "http://www.bigthings.ca/bignb.html"

COFFEE BREAK

- Number of Tim Horton's in Canada: 2,611
- Number of Tim Horton's in New Brunswick: 121

Source: Tim Horton's.

VINO

- Number of wineries in New Brunswick: 9
- Per capita, New Brunswicker's expenditure on wine in 2002/03: $79.60
- The number of litres of wine the average New Brunswickers bought in 2003: 7.7

Sources: Statistics Canada; Tourism New Brunswick.

SEE YOU AT THE FREX

For more than 175 years, the Fredericton Exhibition, or 'the FREX,' has been home to the biggest draft horse show and agricultural exhibition in New Brunswick. The FREX, held each September, includes a provincial cattle show, a petting zoo, daily stage shows, handicrafts, home economics judging and harness racing during its weeklong run. Don't miss the rides at the midway either. The fun also includes a midway, snacks like Dippy Dogs, a FREX treat served up by a local service club, and live entertainment.

Did you know...

that one of the English-speaking world's most favourite games was dreamed up and patented in New Brunswick? Shediac's Edward R. McDonald first put Scrabble on the table in 1926.

IRISH FESTIVAL ON THE MIRAMICHI

The Miramichi's Irish Festival celebrates the province's strong Irish history and traditions by highlighting the still-vibrant Irish culture. Festival-goers can learn to play an Irish whistle, and learn about their Irish heritage with the help of on-sight archives and genealogists. Set against the scenic backdrop of the Miramichi in July, the festival offers the opportunity for everyone to tip a pint and enjoy being Irish, even if only for a day.

ATLANTIC INTERNATIONAL HOT AIR BALLOON FESTIVAL

Held annually each fall, this festival treats visitors to a rainbow of colour as hot air balloons hover over scenic Sussex.

Meanwhile, some of the better-known (and best-kept secret) Maritime performers take centre stage on the bandstand throughout the weekend.

The festival also boasts craft horse show, midway, Fundy model forest, bingo tent, helicopter rides, a model train display, and an Antique Car Show exhibiting hundreds of classic rides.

Weblinks

Beaverbrook Art Gallery
http://www.beaverbrookartgallery.org/index.asp
Find out about the exhibits and other activities happening at this premiere
Art Gallery featuring the work of top Canadian and European artists.

Music/Musique NB
http://www.musicnb.org/
See what's happening on the provincial music scene with this "voice
of the New Brunswick music industry."

New Brunswick Museum
http://www.nbm-mnb.ca/
Read about the museums exhibits and click and learn your way
through its online virtual exhibits.

Tourism New Brunswick
http://www.tourismnewbrunswick.ca/index.htm
Visiting New Brunswick? Find out what's happening when you're here.

Acadian Culture in New Brunswick
http://www.countycrier.com/id53.html
Learn all about Acadian culture in New Brunswick.

Crime and Punishment

CRIMELINE

October 6, 1784: New Brunswick's first murder victim, John Mosley, takes a fatal pitchfork to the head, courtesy of his wife. As punishment she is (literally) branded a murderess.

1784: The first Supreme Court justices are sworn into office and hold their first session.

May 2, 1786: William Lewis and John Ryan are tried in the province's first libel suit. Found guilty, the pair are fined and ordered to bank security in case they do it again.

November 14, 1835: Canada's first asylum for the criminally insane opens in Saint John separating the mentally ill from the criminal.

March 3, 1855: Samuel Leonard Tilley introduces a bill to criminalize liquor. It passes but proves unenforceable and is quickly repealed.

July 15, 1880: The last brick is laid at the new Dominion penitentiary in Dorchester.

April 26, 1909: The owner of the Bijou Moving Picture Theatre in Saint John is tried and found guilty of stealing a brand new commodity – electricity – from the St. John Railway Company.

May 5, 1909: William Parks and Carl Shultz break their chain gang shackles near Saint John. Shultz is picked up immediately; Parks, serving a year for stealing boots, puts them to good use and spends more time on the lamb.

May 1, 1917: Prohibition becomes law. Liquor is illegal except for religious and "medicinal purposes."

September 5, 1918: Canada's first police union is organized in Saint John.

September 24, 1918: A three-year inquiry opens into the Patriotic Potato Scandal, uncovering a stew of political corruption including patronage, bribery and perjury.

October 11, 1918: Gatherings of more than five people are outlawed in an effort to avoid the Spanish flu, a disease that eventually claims more than 50,000 Canadians.

April 20, 1927: Drinkers toast the end of prohibition as the New Brunswick Liquor Control Board is formed and liquor stores open for business.

November 8, 1928: Five men led by George Bulger are caught and arrested for digging a tunnel under the highway between Chatham and Newcastle in search of treasure buried by Captain Kidd.

December 7, 1957: 29-year-old Joseph Pierre Richard is the last man hanged in New Brunswick, executed for the rape and murder of 14-year-old Katherine de la Perelle.

May 3, 1989: Convicted murderer Allan Leger escapes his guards while visiting a Moncton hospital.

November 24, 1989: Allan Legere is captured.

The Monster of the Miramichi

In 1989 Allan Joseph Legere was serving a life sentence for his part in the 1986 beating and rape of shopkeeper Mary Glendenning and the murder of her husband John. That spring, on a routine hospital visit, Legere used a collapsed TV antenna he hid in his rectum and a piece of metal hidden in a cigar to unlock his cuffs and shackles and escape to freedom.

Legere spent the next seven months torturing, raping, burning and killing his way around the region. His innocent victims included 75-year-old Annie Flam, 45 and 41-year-old sisters Donna and Linda Lou Daughney, and 69-year-old Reverend James Smith.

Reported sightings of Legere poured in from across Canada, but the police were certain Legere had remained close to home. One of the largest manhunts in Canadian history ensued – with rewards of up to $50,000 offered for his capture. New Brunswickers were terrified. People armed themselves and avoided going out after dark. That year Halloween festivities were cancelled.

Finally, on November 24th, Legere was captured. His trial turned into a media frenzy, something Legere himself seemed to have enjoyed. The accused went on a hunger strike and successfully appealed to have a book about the case banned. The trial was also one of the first in Canada to use DNA evidence. In the end, Legere was found guilty on four counts of first degree murder and sentenced to life in prison. Legere is currently housed in the maximum security Special Handling Unit in Quebec, home to only about 90 inmates who are the most violent criminals in the country.

The Horror of Kingsclear

When the New Brunswick Training School was opened at Kingsclear in 1962, it was believed that boys in trouble with the law or from broken homes might get the help they needed. For more than 200 boys, Kingsclear became a living hell. The source of their hell was staffer Karl Toft, who began beating, fondling, and raping the school's residents in 1962.

In 1983, a Roman Catholic chaplain told the school's acting superintendent that Toft was committing sexual crimes with the boys under his care. The chaplain was told that not only were his allegations not the first, but they would not be written up in a complaint. Two years later, in October 1985, a youth counsellor witnessed Toft sexually touch a school resident. He reported the incident to school officials and the Fredericton city police, but no inquiries were made and again no action taken.

Toft was transferred to an adult institution adjoining the boys' facility but continued to have access to boys because he was permitted to participate in summer camp programs. In 1990, the former counsellor who had reported Toft's actions five years earlier went to the CBC with his story. The CBC contacted the provincial Attorney General who in turn requested an RCMP investigation.

In 1991, Karl Toft was arrested and charged with sexual offences. He eventually admitted, in 1992, to fondling more than 200 boys. He was charged on only 34 counts and connected to only 18 victims. It is estimated that perhaps the true number of his victims surpasses 1,000.

Karl Toft spent thirteen years in jail for his crime. His 2005 release stirred a massive public outcry from those who believe the pedophile poses a risk to children everywhere. Toft's legal troubles may not be over. In July 2006 a New Brunswick judge ruled that a former victim of Toft's has enough evidence to pursue a private prosecution case.

November 3, 1991: Thanks to DNA evidence, Allan Legere is found guilty of four murders he committed while on the lamb. Convicted, he becomes one of the fewer than 100 people housed in the nation's Special Handling Unit.

April 25, 2005: Gregory Depres is alleged to have murdered his two elderly neighbours and fled to the United States. The blood-spattered fugitive makes international news when he somehow manages to slip through U.S. customs with a cache of weapons.

April 26, 2005: The bodies of 74 year old Fred Fulton and his common-law wife, 70 year-old Verna Decarie, Depres' alleged victims, are found in their modest Minto home.

April 27, 2005: Depres is arrested in Mattapoisett, Massachusetts and charged with murder. Later extradited to Canada, at the time of printing he awaits trial.

December 2, 2005: Convicted pedophile Karl Toft is freed after serving time in prison on 34 counts of sexual assault committed at the Kingsclear Youth Training Centre near Fredericton.

OUTLAWING LIQUOR

Before the mid nineteenth century, booze was a staple in New Brunswick trade. Bells rang out telling workers it was time for their rum break. Paychecks were paid in liquid form. And political palms

Did you know...

that the government controlled post-prohibition liquor with an iron fist? The only legal drink on tap in the province for thirty years after it went 'wet' was in liquor stores. The government refused during that time to license any public watering holes.

were greased with boozey bribes.

In the mid 19th century, however, the province was caught up in the temperance wave that swept the U.S. and Canada. The devil's juice was reckoned to be at the root of just about every social evil on the planet, and people of all walks of life united to criminalize drink and clean up society.

Taking its lead from the state of Maine, New Brunswick was one of the first British colonies to prohibit drink – as early as 1855 booze was banned, albeit briefly. By WWI, "going dry" became an act of patriotism and in 1917 liquor was again made illegal. This time the law stuck for a decade until, in 1927, prohibition ended and the provincial Liquor Control Board began to control and market alcohol.

BETWEEN THE DEVIL AND THE DEEP BLUE SEA

As the burning embers of the temperance movement sparked prohibition in the early 20th century in New Brunswick, the province became part of what continues to this day to be an Atlantic Canada tradition: rum smuggling. Although it did not run the same volume as its Maritime neighbours, what New Brunswick lacked in volume it more than made up for in variety.

Coastal islands such as Campobello offered cloaked shelter for 'wet' goods arriving from Holland, France, Scotland and Ireland – not to mention from local stills — before they turned into forbidden riches on their way to the coastal U.S. and the rest of Canada. Today, New Brunswick, along with the other Atlantic Provinces, is still an integral jumping point for illicit products moving in and out of the country.

They Said It

"I don't usually comment on verdicts . . . but let me say this: don't lose too much sleep over your verdict."

— Justice David Dickson, commenting on the jury's verdict in the Allan Legere murder tria

A WET HOUSE

Even after prohibition was ended, illegal booze manufacture remained an economic sideline for enterprising New Brunswickers. Sasha's Lounge in Moncton and a secret corridor in its basement are reminders of the ongoing battle between the government and moonshiners.

Carl Doull, who owned the property in the 1920s, enjoyed boot-legged drink and the profits that could be wrung from it. Legend has it that Doull's building was raided several times, by government liquor control officials. Countless times Doull out-smarted the officers and their searches came up empty. In the early weeks of 1929, however, Doull's luck ran out. Deep in the recesses of the secret hallway officials found 1,000 gallons of bootleg liquor.

Doull was arrested and charged with holding liquor neither distilled nor distributed by the Control Board. He was jailed for six months and fined $500. He served his time at the Dorchester County Jail where he and other liquor "entrepreneurs" were, not surprisingly, accorded preferential treatment.

MURDER

- The number of murders in New Brunswick in 2004: 7
- In the rest of Canada: 622
- The murder rate in New Brunswick in 2004: 0.9 per 100,000
- In the rest of Canada: 2.0 per 100,000
- Number of unsolved major crimes in New Brunswick: 24 (17 murders, 3 suspicious deaths, 3 missing persons and 1 home invasion)

Source: Statistics Canada.

Did you know...

that Allan Legere was the first serial killer in Canada to be convicted by DNA typing?

Take 5 TOP FIVE CRIMES
COMMITTED IN NEW BRUNSWICK

1. **Theft under $5,000**
2. **Assault**
3. **Break and Enter**
4. **Traffic Offences**
5. **Motor Vehicle Theft**

Source: Statistics Canada.

CRIMES BY THE NUMBER

- Number of criminal code incidents recorded in New Brunswick in 2004: 54,993
- Rate of criminal code incidents recorded in New Brunswick in 2004: 7313 per 100,000
- Rate of criminal code incidents recorded in Canada in 2004: 8051 per 100,000

DOING TIME

- Number of adults admitted to correctional facilities in 2003: 4,321
- Number of adults given probation and conditional sentences in 2003: 2,368
- Number of youths admitted to correctional facilities in 2003: 74
- Number of youths given probation and community supervision in 2003: 654
- Incarceration rate for youth in New Brunswick in 2003: 0.13 per 10,000

Did you know...

that alcohol plays a role in 31 percent of all fatal crashes in New Brunswick?

Take 5 TOP FIVE MOST COMMON
VEHICLES STOLEN IN NEW BRUNSWICK

1. Vans
2. Pick-up Trucks
3. All Terrain Vehicles (ATVs)
4. Heavy Equipment
5. Trailers and Transport Trucks

Source: Government of New Brunswick.

- Number of crimes committed in New Brunswick involving youth in 2003: 1,434

Source: Statistics Canada.

CRIME IN SAINT JOHN

In 2005, Saint John recorded a total of 6,713 crimes per 100,000 citizens. This is far fewer than the crime rate of 13,236 per 100,000 recorded in Saskatoon, the nation's most crime-ridden city.

Saint John
Homicide: 0 per 100,000
Robberies: 44 per 100,000
Break-ins: 522 per 100,000
Motor-vehicle theft: 137 per 100,000

Source: Statistics Canada.

Nation's highest
Edmonton, 4.3 per 100,000
Winnipeg, 263 per 100,000
Regina, 1,740 per 100,000
Winnipeg, 1,712 per 100,000

Did you know...

that the most popular counterfeit bills passed in New Brunswick are the 20- and 50- dollar denominations? They are followed by the $10 bill and the $100. Together the bills added up to about 36,000 fake dollars passed in 2004.

IN 2004 NEW BRUNSWICK HAD:

- 7 homicides
- 5,705 assaults
- 253 robberies
- 1,828 motor vehicle thefts
- 361 thefts over $5,000
- 12,064 thefts under $5,000
- 5,355 break and enters
- 608 sexual assaults
- 2758 traffic offences
- 242 mischief cases

Source: Statistics Canada.

AVERAGE JOE OFFENDER

- Average age of offenders in New Brunswick: 30
- Average sentence: 18 days

Source: Statistics Canada.

TO SERVE AND PROTECT

- Number of police officers in New Brunswick: 1,297 or 172 per 100,000 citizens
- Nationally, as of 2005, there are 61,050 police officers, or 189 per 100,000 Canadians.

Source: Statistics Canada.

Take 5 TOP FIVE DRUGS
USED ILLEGALLY IN NEW BRUNSWICK

1. **Cannabis Products** (Marijuana, Hashish and Hashish Oil)
2. **Cocaine**
3. **Ecstasy**
4. **Oxycontin**
5. **Dilaudid**

Source: Government of New Brunswick.

FAKIN' IT

- In 2005 number of counterfeit bank notes passed in New Brunswick: 899
- Number of fake notes seized by police in New Brunswick: 173 (19 percent)
- Number passed nationally in the same year: 417,825
- Number seized nationally: 22,588 (5 percent)

Source: RCMP.

INCARCERATION

A quarter of the 6,772 people convicted in New Brunswick in 2003 did time for their crimes while another 8.5 percent received a conditional sentence. Nearly 40 percent of those found guilty were given probation. In Canada, the same year saw 257,127 convicted with 35 percent being incarcerated, 5.2 percent receiving a conditional sentence and 46 percent walking away on probation.

- Incarceration rates in New Brunswick: 52 per 100,000
- Incarceration rates in Canada: 130 per 100,000
- Probation rates in New Brunswick: 353 per 100,000
- Probation rates in Canada: 311 per 100,000
- Percentage of offenders who end up in jail: 25
- Average median sentence: 60 days
- Percentage of sentences less than a month: 65
- Percentage spending more than 12 months behind bars: 3.8

Source: Statistics Canada.

They Said It

"The measure of the failure of these officials is the fact that not one of them even asked questions as to the age or identity of the victims. Not one of them even appeared to care."

— Comments of The Hon. Richard L. Miller, Chair of the Inquiry established to investigate the abuse at the Kingsclear facility.

Did you know...

STOLEN IDENTITY

It's not just cars and wallets that get stolen in New Brunswick. In 2005, 127 people complained of stolen identities and it cost them $29,107.52. Nationally, there were a total of 11,231 complaints of ID theft, which cost Canadians over $8.5 million.

Source: RCMP.

IT'LL COST YA

Each day it costs $114.21 to incarcerate an inmate – working out to $42,686.65 a year.

Source: Statistics Canada.

DRUG CRIME

In 2003, 522 people were convicted of drug related offences in New Brunswick. Of those, 355 were picked up for holding something, while 197 were picked up for trying to sell it to someone else. Just about 100 of those convicted did time; nearly the same amount of offenders received conditional sentences, while 130 others got probation. One of the biggest problems facing drug enforcement in the province today is marijuana grow operations.

- The number of grow operations busted in New Brunswick in 2004: 437
- Value of busted 2004 grow operations: $38 million

Source: RCMP.

Did you know...

TAKING A BITE OUT OF CRIME

CrimeStoppers has been working for more than two decades to take a bite out of New Brunswick's crime. Since 1985 the group has been instrumental in solving 6,587 cases, laying 7,527 charges, arresting 7,451 people, recovering over $6 million in stolen property, confiscating nearly $33 million in drugs and even in bringing 272 fugitives to justice. All this for a little more than a half a million dollars seems like a pretty great deal.

Source: CrimeStoppers.

Weblinks

HER MAJESTY THE QUEEN - and - ALLAN JOSEPH LEGERE:
A Digital Archive
http://law.unb.ca/library/legere.draft.htm
Check out this site by the Gerard V. La Forest Law Library, University of New Brunswick. Here you can read all about Allan Legere's reign of terror, and even read the transcript of his trial.

Royal Canadian Mounted Police
http://www.rcmp-grc.gc.ca/nb/index_e.htm
Visit this site to find out what the RCMP are up to in New Brunswick. Here you can see the organization's priorities, plans and programs for preventing crime in the province.

New Brunswick Public Safety
http://www.gnb.ca/0276/index-e.asp
This is home to the Government of New Brunswick's Department of Public Safety. Here you can find out about crime in the province and what the government is doing to curb it. The site also offers tips and tricks to avoid becoming a victim.

First People

PRE-ENCOUNTER

Because New Brunswick's first people spent much of their time along coasts and rivers, most of the artifacts and material remains of their ancient settlements have been washed away or destroyed by erosion. Surviving archaeological sites suggest that New Brunswick's first people have inhabited the province for tens of thousands of years. In fact, some 20,000 years ago, when much of North America was covered by ice, it is likely that people were living in this region.

More concrete is the evidence that by 11,000 years ago people — known by archaeologists as Paleo-Indians —were living in the Maritimes. The walrus, then common on the east coast of North America, were an important resource for Paleo-Indians. For some reason, though, Paleo-Indians people ceased to exist and came to be replaced by a group known as the Maritime archaic people.

For 3,500 to 4,500 years, they relied predominantly on sea resources, though some lived inland, notably around Grand Lake. Then, about 2,500 years ago, a whole new people moved to the province, likely from the Ohio Valley, to settle along the Miramichi. The use of ceramic pots was a particularly noteworthy, if short-lived characteristic of these people. By the time of encounter, lightweight, portable and durable birch bark vessels and European copper kettles were in use, likely preceding the arrival of Europeans in the area through trade.

CREATION

The Mi'kmaq, Maliseet and Pasamaquoddy people believe that the universe was created by a Great Spirit. Called Gluskap by the Mi'kmaq, and Koluskap by the Maliseet and Passamaquoddy, this cultural hero is believed to have created everything. The Great Spirit has no gender and people do not seek to explain the Spirit's origins. What is important is that this Great Spirit created everything.

Maliseet-Passamaquoddy Dictionary

man	Skitap
Woman	Ehpit
Dog	Olomuss
Sun	Kisuhs
Moon	Kisuhs, Nipawset
Water	'Samaqan
White	Wapi
Yellow	Wisawi
Red	Mqeyu or Pqeyu
Black	Mokosewi
Eat	Mitsu
See	Nomihtu
Hear	Nutomon
Sing	Lintu
Leave	Nokotomon or Macehe

ENCOUNTER

When the first Europeans arrived in New Brunswick, the Mi'kmaq lived in the northeastern region, the Maliseet throughout the St. John River Valley and the Passamaquoddy in the southeastern reaches along what is now the Maine-New Brunswick border. At the time of first encounter, there were an estimated 10,000 to 35,000 Mi'kmaq and Maliseet and a few hundred Passamaquoddy. Within 500 years their numbers had been decimated by up to between percent.

THE MI'KMAQ

The Mi'kmaq know themselves as L'nu'k, or "the people" and their language is Mi'kmawi'simk. The Mi'kmaq were probably the first New Brunswickers to encounter Europeans. In July 1534, when Jacques Cartier sailed into and named Chaleur Bay, he was greeted by a contingent of Mi'kmaq who motioned their interest in trading with the European sailors. It was clear they had traded before.

At the time of encounter, the Mi'kmaq lived a mobile life based on the seasons, spending summer months along the coast and moving inland during the winter. Their homes were portable, conical wigwams.

MALISEET

The Maliseet know themselves as the Wolastoqiyik, or "the people of the beautiful river," a reference to the St. John River. Their language is also called Wolastoqiyik. It is believed that prior to encounter the Maliseet lived year round along the coast in sturdy permanent homes.

Sometime just before Europeans arrived, the Maliseet began to relocate to inland areas during winters. This may have been the result of the changing availability of natural resources or the effects of indirect European influence. It was around the same time that the Mi'kmaq also began to live in conical wigwams. Probably to a greater extent than the Mi'kmaq, the Maliseet engaged in agriculture.

THE PASSAMAQUODDY

The Passamaquoddy know themselves as the Pestomuhkatiyik, or "the people of the pollock-spearing place," namely Passamaquoddy Bay. At the time of European encounter, the Passamaquoddy lived in south-western New Brunswick and Maine, around the bay and along the St. Croix River. They were relatives of, and allies to, the Maliseet, with whom they shared a dialect.

Like the Maliseet, the Pasamaquoddy lived along the coast year round. Their homes were partially dug in the ground and protected from

Treaty Timeline

The first people of New Brunswick signed at least eleven treaties (commonly known as "Peace and Friendship Treaties) with the British." The British were motivated to enter into treaty in order to end intermittent conflict between themselves and the politically powerful first people. In exchange for peace and the respect of civil and criminal law, the Mi'kmaq, Maliseet and Pasamaquoddy were promised continued hunting and fishing rights and the free-dom of their Roman Catholic religion. Significantly, these treaties saw the first people cede no land to the British.

Treaty of 1725-26 The so-called Dummer's Treaty, it was negotiated in Boston by the Mi'kmaq and the British in 1725 and ratified by the Mi'kmaq and Maliseet in 1726. It was renewed in 1749.

Treaty of 1752 Signed by Jean Baptiste Cope, a Mi'kmaq from eastern Nova Scotia, and the Governor of Nova Scotia. The agreement made peace, and guaranteed the Mi'kmaq rights to hunt, fish and trade.

Treaties of 1760-61 Signed by the Governor of Nova Scotia and representatives of the Mi'kmaq, Maliseet and Passamaquoddy people. These granted First People the right to fish and harvest fruit and berries. The Mi'kmaq promised not to harass the British. They did not cede land.

the elements by bark and skins. Their main village, Qonasqamkuk, which served as a meeting place and burial ground, was located at the site of modern day St. Andrews. They probably greeted Champlain in 1604 when he sailed up the St. Croix in his attempt at settlement.

The Passamaquoddy provided refuge to fleeing Loyalists in the 1780s, though the favour was not returned; shortly thereafter, the Loyalists forced the Passamaquoddy off their land. Today a small number of Pasamaquoddy live in Charlotte County, where they are actively engaged in land claims and a fight for recognition. They are not officially recognized as a Canadian First Nation.

NEW BRUNSWICK FIRST NATIONS TODAY
In 2001, 16,990 New Brunswickers were of aboriginal descent: 11,495 had Indian status, 4,290 were Métis and 155 were Inuit.

Federally recognized Maliseet Communities

	Population
Madawaska Maliseet First Nation	230
Kingsclear	837
Oromoncto	496
St. Mary's	1,295
Tobique	1,888
Woodstock	801
Total:	5,547

Federally recognized Mi'kmaq Communities

	Population
Fort Folly	105
Buctouche	97
Elsipogtog First Nation (Big Cove)	2,784
Indian Island	148
Metepenagiag Mi'kmaq Nation	529
Eel Ground Branch	860

Burnt Church	1,550
Pabineau Band	250
Eel River	599
Total:	6,922

Source: Indian and Northern Affairs.

FIRST NATION MI'KMAQ AND MALISEET PLACE NAMES AND THEIR MEANINGS

Apohaqui (*Maliseet*): the junction of two streams

Aukpaque (*Maliseet*): where the tide stops coming in

Chiputneticook (*Passamaquoddy*): great fork river

Cobscook (*Maliseet*): at the falls

Keswick (*Maliseet*): where water flows over soft gravel

Kouchibouguac (*Mi'kmaq*): river of the long tides

Mactaquac (*Maliseet*): where the river is red

Magaguadavic Lake (*Maliseet/Passamaquoddy*): river of big eels

Manawagonish Cove (*Maliseet*): a place of clams

Napadogan (*Maliseet*): brook to be followed

Neguac (*Mi'kmaq*): springs out of the ground

Pokemouche (*Mi'kmaq*): salt water extending inland

Quispamsis (*Maliseet*): little lake

Restigouche (*Mi'kmaq*): nicely flowing river

Tabusintac (*Mi'kmaq*): a pair of them (probably referring to rivers)**Aukpaque** (*Maliseet*): where the tide stops coming in

Wolastook (*Maliseet*):   beautiful river

SPIRITUAL TRADITIONS

Like many aboriginals, the first people of New Brunswick are animistic and believe humans to be part of a multi-layered universe in which all animals and objects have a spiritual essence. The physical and spiritual worlds interact continuously. This philosophy informs the belief among the Mi'kmaq, Maliseet and Passamoquoddy that all parts of a killed animal must be preserved and respected. Failure to respect the animal might result in hunting scarcity.

People are not isolated from the spirit world, and some can communicate with it. The Mi'kmaq call such a person a puion, while the Maliseet and Pasamaquoddy refer to a spirit communicator as a motewolon. Aided by a medicine bag containing sacred items such as bones, pebbles and carvings, these spirit guides communicate with the spirit world to learn the locations of game and fish and predict the weather.

POLITICS

Sagamores were the political leaders of the first people of New Brunswick. Known as saqamaws by the Mi'kmaq and sakoms by the Maliseet and Passamaquoddy, sagamores were men chosen by a community to advise them in political matters. Sometimes a sagamore's position was handed down from father to son or uncle to cousin, but merit was more important, and a sagamore had to prove his worth as a leader.

One way he could do this was by sharing the spoils of his hunting with his whole community, ensuring their collective well-being. A sagamore did not rule dictatorially or autocratically. Instead, political decisions were made using persuasion and consensus.

THE MI'KMAQ GRAND COUNCIL

The Mi'kmaq homeland, Mi'kma'ki, spanned Atlantic Canada and was divided into seven districts. In New Brunswick, the district of Siknikt (meaning which means "drainage place") encompassed Nova

They Said It

"Every culture has a right to tell its own story. I have produced my work in the shadows of the cultural hegemony of American and Canadian media giants without giving up the basic teachings of my past. I would like to be known as a person who is here to help create cinema that is by us, for us, about us!"

— Jeff Bear, Maliseet film producer

Scotia's Cumberland county as well as New Brunswick's Westmoreland, Albert, Kent, St. John's, Kings and Queens counties. Kespek, the "last land," stretched out across northern New Brunswick, north of the Richibucto River and into Quebec.

Each of the seven territories had a district sagamore. Several times a year these sagamores would travel to Cape Breton for gatherings of the Grand Council, or the Sante' Mawiomi. This region-wide political body was (and remains) responsible for the spiritual and political well being of the Mi'kmaq. Today, local communities, rather than districts, are represented in the Grand Council by elected captains.

WABANAKI CONFEDERACY

The Wabanaki Confederacy is a political alliance consisting of the Natives of northeastern North America. Meaning "Dawnland People," the Wabanaki alliance included the Penobscot (of present day Maine), Passamaquoddy, Maliseet and Mi'kmaq. The Confederacy was established in the 17th century in response to the political and military threat posed by enemy Iroquois.

The Confederacy met to preserve peace, develop concerted political and military strategies, and negotiate with other Natives and Europeans. It also served as a cultural connector between these First Nations. In 1862, the Wabanaki Confederacy officially disbanded, although informal alliances between these nations continue the Wabanaki relationship.

Did you know...

that New Brunswick First Nations can cross freely between the United States and Canada? This right was granted them in the 1794 Jay's Treaty that established the boundary between New Brunswick and the state of Maine.

MALISEET GATHERING PLACE

Today's Kingsclear, located on the St. John River just above Fredericton, was a traditional spring gathering place of the Maliseet. Known by the Maliseet as Aukapque, or "head of tide," this site was particularly important because it was home to seasonal spawning runs of salmon and bass.

WAMPUM

Before and after Europeans arrived in North America, New Brunswick's first people traded and had diplomatic relations with people across the continent. Wampum, belts strung with beads of purple and white shell, was central to these exchanges. Known as wapap ("white string") by the Maliseet (meaning "white string") or waiopsgug by the Mi'kmaq ("beads"), the arrangement of beads on each belt could transmit any number of messages. They might signify a peace alliance or a treaty, a political agreement, demonstrate an individual's importance, or even make a marriage proposal.

MALISEET TRAIL

The first people of New Brunswick had a system of 'highways' that carried them through dense forests and along rivers. The Maliseet trail is one such route. This pathway, which consisted of 200 kilometers of paddling along the St. John, St. Croix and Penobscot Rivers and 20 more kilometers of portaging, cut through the interior of the province. It connected the Maliseet centre of Medoctec to Indian Island, near present-day Old Town, Maine.

Did you know...

that in 1971 Margaret LaBillois of Eel River Bar became the first female chief in New Brunswick? In 1998, she received the Order of Canada followed by the Order of New Brunswick in 2005.

A MI'KMAQ CREATION STORY: SUGAR LOAF MOUNTAIN

A long time ago, the Mi'kmaq living on riverbanks noticed that salmon could no longer go up the river to spawn. They discovered that beavers, which were very large then, had built a dam across the Restigouche River thus preventing the passage of the salmon. This upset the Mi'kmaq, who needed the salmon to survive.

The men tried to break up the dams, but the beavers used their tails to upset the men in their canoes. The men swam to shore and called on the loon to summon Koluskap, who came to them riding on the back of his whale. The Mi'kmaq explained what the beaver had done.

Bio SENATOR SANDRA LOVELACE NICHOLAS

The Indian Act is considered by many to be racist legislation aimed at controlling the lives of Canada's First Nations. It is also considered sexist, as it one time declared that any Native woman who married a non-Native man would lose her status as an 'Indian' as well as any status rights conferred by the Act. Her children would also be denied status. A Native man, however, could marry a woman of any background and maintain his status, which was then transferred to his spouse and children.

In 1985, the Indian Act was revised and this discriminatory clause removed, thanks to a New Brunswick woman. Maliseet Sandra Lovelace was born on the Tobique reserve in 1948. As a young woman, she moved to California where she married and divorced a non-Native man. When she returned to Tobique in the 1970s, she found herself denied her Native status and rights. A movement to oust this section of the Indian Act was already underway, and Lovelace joined the fight in 1977 by taking her case to the Human Rights Committee of the United Nations.

Late in 1979 the UN allowed the Canadian government to defend its support of the discriminatory section of the Act. Ottawa argued,

Koluskap walked on the dam and in the centre he used a club to hit it. Parts of the dam went flying, forming islands and other areas of land.

Koluscap then caught the leader of the beaver. Grabbing him by the tail, he swung the beaver and let go, sending the animal flying. When the beaver landed, far away, he turned to rock. This rock is known as Sugar Loaf Mountain. Koluskap then returned to the rest of the beavers. To soothe the frightened animals, he stroked their heads. With each stroke, they shrunk, eventually to the size they are today. Koluskap promised the Mi'kmaq that the beavers would never grow large again and never again dam their river.

with some validity, that most Natives opposed changing the Act for fear that the rights granted by it may, too, be challenged. The UN did not accept this argument and Native women were pleased when it found Canada in breach of the 1981 International Covenant on Civil and Political Rights.

Canada was essentially shamed into action, and in 1985 the Indian Act was finally changed. Native women who married non-Native men, and their children, would no longer lose their status and those who previously lost it, had it reinstated. Lovelace's contribution to women's rights did not go unnoticed. For her contribution to the fight, in 1990 Lovelace became a Member of the Order of Canada and in 1992 she won the Governor General's Award in Commemoration of the Persons Case in 1992.

Sandra Lovelace Nicholas has four children, a degree in residential construction from the Maine Northern Technical College, and is a carpenter. In September 2005, Prime Minster Paul Martin appointed her to the senate. More than twenty years after she succeeded in changing the Indian Act, she continues to be an activist for women's and aboriginal rights.

OXBOW SITE

Touted as the oldest continuously inhabited community in Canada, the Oxbow Site, located at Red Bank on the Southwest Miramichi River, contains evidence of a fishing village that has existed for more than 3,000 years.

Called Metepenagiag by the Mi'kmaq, it is not only home to fabulous fishing and fish spawning grounds, it is also located at a convenient midway point between the coastal Mi'kmaq fishery and inland hunting grounds. Although the coming of Europeans diminished fishing stocks, life at Metepenagiag continues to revolve around this ancient fishery. The Oxbow site is a National Historic Site and is being developed into a Heritage Park.

AUGUSTINE MOUND

In 1972, as Joseph M. Augustine was reading an article about an ancient Arizona burial ground, he was reminded of a similar mound that his father had shown him years before at Red Bank. His curiosity piqued, Augustine began to excavate the site and found a treasure trove of artifacts. When archaeologists heard of his discovery they investigated and named the incredible archaeological site after its discoverer.

The Augustine mound yielded unprecedented information about the ancestors of the Mi'kmaq. The items unearthed, including cremations, burials, beads, copper and basketry, proved that the Mi'kmaq had lived on that site for more than 2,000 years. The items also connected the ancient inhabitants of the southwest Miramichi with the Adena culture from the Ohio Valley, offering new information about the prehistory of New Brunswick's first people.

Did you know...

that only the treaties of 1760-61 and the treaty of 1752 have been formally recognized as treaties by the Supreme Court of Canada?

HOLIDAYS IN MI'KMAQ

Puna'ne'wimk - New Year's Day

Mnumkwej Na'kwekm - Ground Hog Day

Kesaltultimkewey Na'kwek - Valentine's Day

Pa'tliksite'wimk - St. Patrick's Day

Na'qatpa'ltimk Na'kwek - April Fool's Day

L'nuk Nakwekmuew - National Aboriginal Day (June 21)

Se't A'newimk - St. Anne's Day (July 26, the Mi'kmaq annual holiday)

Kisaknutmamkewey Na'kwek - Treaty Day (October 1)

Skitekmujuia'timk - Hallowe'en

Nepkik Alasutmelsewujik - Prayers for the Dead - All Saints Day

Sma'knis Na'kwekm - Remembrance Day

Nipialasutmamk - Christmas Day

Poqtamkiaq Pestie'wa'taqatimk - Boxing Day

BURNT CHURCH (ESGENOOPETITJ)

In 1999, the Supreme Court of Canada's Marshall decision recognized the treaty right of the Mi'kmaq to fish for profit, out of season, and without license. Native and non-native fishers alike have hotly contested the exact meaning of this ruling. Immediately following the ruling, 34 Mi'kmaq bands in the Maritimes and eastern Quebec instituted an out-of-season lobster fishery.

Non-native fishers were angered and demanded Ottawa stop the catch. New Brunswick's Burnt Church became the flashpoint in the dispute. On October 3, 1999, non-Native fishers congregated in Miramichi Bay to protest the native fishery. Native fishers were outraged when protestors vandalized hundreds of their traps, along with three fish plants.

Did you know...

that Maliseet T.J. Burke is Atlantic Canada's first aboriginal MLA? He was elected for the riding of Fredericton North in the 2003 provincial election.

Guarded by Mi'kmaq warriors, the fishery continued. Three days later, most Atlantic Canadian First Nations agreed to a voluntary moratorium. Though tensions were calmed, Burnt Church and Indian Brook refused to concede their fishing rights. In November 1999, a request for a rehearing of an appeal was denied, but in an unprecedented move, a new Supreme Court ruling, known as Marshall 2, was issued to clarify the original decision. Significantly, Marshall 2 empowered Ottawa to regulate fishing for conservation.

A winter of discussions saw a federal plan emerge. Ottawa planned to buy back commercial lobster licenses in order to expand the Native fishery. By the summer of 2000, fishermen had agreed to sell back more than 5,000 licenses. By August 2000, all First Nations but Burnt Church and Indian Brook had inked agreements containing guidelines for the coming season's fishery. These two communities continued to fish, insisting they could regulate their own fisheries.

The federal Department of Fisheries and Oceans took action, seizing boats and arresting Native fishers. Tensions reached an all time high. About 700 Native traps were seized and DFO officials were accused of using brute force on Miramichi Bay. Natives responded with a highway blockade.

In hopes of avoiding a similar scenario for the 2001 season, Burnt Church was allocated a temporary license while a permanent deal was

They Said It

"The agreement was entered into under duress. The government of Canada used our hunger and poverty, violence against us, our vulnerable position, the threats of the Crown, the charges against all of our people who were defending our rights, as coercion against us. All this was used to get our people to 'agree' to a fishery agreement that the community did not want."

— August 27, 2002 Statement from Hereditary
Chief of the Mi'kmaq Grand Council, on Burnt Church

negotiated. Burnt Church, however, refused to endorse the deal, which denied them the right to sell their catches commercially, and imposed an August 27 closure date for the fishery.

On August 26, 2001, tensions were high in anticipation of Ottawa's deadline. All roads to the Burnt Church First Nation were blocked. Ottawa extended the deadline and the rest of the season passed without major incident. In the spring of 2002, Ottawa released a report about the Burnt Church dispute. It recommended that all charges laid in the 2001 mêlée on Miramichi Bay be dropped and that Native fishers be compensated for lost traps and boats. That August an agreement-in-principal, worth about $20 million over two years, was reached between Burnt Church and Ottawa.

Weblinks

Wolastoqiyik - Portrait of A People
http://www.gnb.ca/0007/heritage/virtual_exibition/Portraits/Welcome.htm
Containing images of the Wolastoqiyik, or Maliseet, this online exhibit chronicles life, past and present, of life along the Wolastoq (Saint John) river.

Mi'gmaq-Mi'kmaq On-line
http://www.mikmaqonline.org/
This interactive website is a talking dictionary project that features more than 6,000 Mi'kmaq words.

Burnt Church Fishery
http://www.nben.ca/aboutus/caucus/archived_caucuses/ffa_archive/fishery/1_bc_e.htm
This website brings together a wide range of on-line resources concerning the Burnt Church fishery.

Take five more

As you can probably tell, we are partial to things you can count on one hand. This chapter is just more of that. It is designed to be fun, entertaining and insightful, not only in details about the province, but about the person making the choices. It is a chapter that could have continued beyond the bounds of this book. New Brunswickers, famous and not so famous, were literally bursting at the seams with opinion about their province. This means, of course, we'll include more next time.

TAKE 5: CHEF ROSS MAVIS' FIVE FAVOURITE NEW BRUNSWICK INGREDIENTS

Ross Mavis definitely knows cooking. The New Westminster, B.C., native is chef and owner of the Inn on the Cove & Spa in Saint John. Mavis is a world-class talent and one of New Brunswick's most celebrated chefs. Mavis and his wife, Willa, have produced and hosted 135 half-hour episodes of a popular TV cooking show called Tide's Table and have published two cookbooks- Tide's Table -Maritime Cooking from Inn on the Cove and Outdoor Cooking from Tide's Table. With more than 10 years of chef experience in Saint John, Mavis has won many fans with his fabulous dishes. Those fans include The Globe and Mail, The Boston Globe and TV and radio personality Vicki Gabereau. Mavis shares his five favourite New Brunswick ingredients.

1. **Maple Syrup:** New Brunswick Maple Syrup is tops for pancakes and French Toast. It's also wonderful for sweet / spicy glazes for entrées, such as CraNew Brunswickerry glazed Cornish Hen, Duck Breast a l'Orange or maple mustard glazed Ham Hocks. The New Brunswick maple product I use is Certified Organic and is consistently of excellent quality. How sweet it is.

2. **St. John River Valley Apples:** St. John River Valley apples and apple products from Gagetown are excellent for spa lunches and main menu desserts. Apple cheddar crepes make an exciting breakfast alternate, especially when napped with New Brunswick Maple Cream sauce. Sweet apple cider is a winner when used in baked beans with pork.

3. **Bay of Fundy lobster:** Any superlative is always found wanting when it comes to praising New Brunswick's Bay of Fundy Lobster. This king of seafood is best when straight out of the cold pristine waters off Dipper Harbour. Although there are dozens of ways to prepare this regal delight, simply boiled in correctly salted water and enjoyed with freshly drawn butter and fresh lemon cannot be topped.

4. **Kennebecasis River Fiddleheads:** Kennebecasis River Fiddleheads are a treat we enjoy fresh. I never freeze or pickle this delicious wild vegetable as they are best lightly boiled. buttered, salted and drenched in fresh lemon juice. Tasting like wild asparagus, this seasonal treat must be eaten when freshly picked — so don't dally when spring freshet waters drop.

5. **Grand Manan Dulse:** Grand Manan Dulse is without question the best in the world. I love the way this sea vegetable makes a seafood chowder or fresh pasta with mussels and cream sauce taste so briny and reminiscent of the mighty tides that surge twice daily in and out of the Bay of Fundy. It's a treat to eat out of hand or dried and used as a condiment.

TAKE 5: GARDENER DUNCAN KELBAUGH'S FIVE FAVOURITE NEW BRUNSWICK PLANTS

When it comes to gardening, Duncan Kelbaugh is the man many people turn to for advice. This owner of Brunswick Nurseries Ltd. in Quispamsis and garden columnist for the Saint John Telegraph Journal, has for years shared his garden knowledge with people from across New Brunswick. Kelbaugh's passion for gardening is contagious. He has helped many find their "inner gardener." Kelbaugh shares five of his favourite New Brunswick plants.

1. **The Ostrich Fern**, commonly known as 'fiddleheads', appeals to me in so many ways. As a canoeist from the Green River in the northwest, to the Kennebecasis River in the southeast, I have picked and boiled fresh fiddleheads most of my life. They make a lovely shade garden plant, have great ornamental value, and make for delish eating. In a province so rich in rivers, this quintessential floodplain-dweller is an important part of our heritage.

2. **Highbush cranberry makes superb jelly**. My Mum would pick pails of them each fall, and the delicious smell of hot berries dripping through cheesecloth would fill the house for hours. There is no better complement to wild duck dinner. The flat sprays of pure white flowers grace our woodlands in spring, then five months later, turn to heavy clusters of bright red berries, accenting the warm tones of sugar and red maple.

3. To happen upon a **trillium** in bloom is always a treat, as they lead their solitary lives in the cool, moist under-story of hardwoods. The red flower, its parts in threes, which inspired the name, stands boldly upright in a shady world of little colour. Don't bother to bend over for a sniff though; you'll be disappointed. Its pungent smell is designed to attract crawling pollinators who mistake it for carrion.

4. **Yellow birch** is the strong, silent, and healthier cousin of white birch. The papery bark has a golden glow in young specimens. This birch is long-lived (100 years +), disease and insect free, and has higher quality wood than its white cousin, making great lumber or fire wood. The tender young twigs when chewed have a telltale taste of wintergreen, unique to this lovely hardwood.

5. **Red spruce** can reach nearly 100 feet in height, with straight branch-free trunks in the older stands. This was a key member of the traditional Acadian Forest, now much diminished by repeated logging and fires. Its seedlings are extremely shade tolerant, lying in wait for decades in the understory, then bursting into rapid growth when the sunlight pours in after logging or blowdown. Along with its forest mates, white pine and hemlock, these are the redwoods of New Brunswick, and deserve our protection and respect

TAKE 5: THE TWO FAT GUYS' TOP FIVE ALTERNATIVE PLACES TO EAT IN NEW BRUNSWICK (IN NO PARTICULAR ORDER)

Bob Morton and Jack LeBlanc are better as The Two Fat Guys. In a regular column appearing in Moncton's edition of Here: New Brunswick's Urban Voice, they share with readers their culinary exploits and gastronomical discoveries as they review New Brunswick restaurants. To read some of their reviews, you can visit Here online at http://www.herenb.com/.

1. **The Gasthof Old Bavarian, in Knightville**, is like no other restaurant in New Brunswick. In fact, its nearest equal is probably in Germany! The food is spectacular, but the setting, in a rustic and rugged chalet-style restaurant, surrounded by cattle and other farm animals, will leave you with the impression you've actually been transported to Deutschland.

2. **The Dinner Theatres at Le Pays de la Sagouine**, in Bouctouche, are a terrific way to spend an evening. The food is great, the entertainment is top notch and guests are immersed in the fictional (sometimes funny and often moving) lives of famous Acadian characters inspired by Antonine Maillet's award-winning book La Sagouine.

3. **The W.W. Boyce Farmer's Market** is the crème de la crème when it comes to farmers' markets. Since 1951, dozens of vendors have gathered at the corner of Regent and George Streets in Fredericton on Saturday mornings to offer up tasty treats of ethnic foods, sweets, meats, as well as crafts and other items. This is a place any self-respecting New Brunswicker has to visit at least once.

4. **The Sugar Bush "La Causerie", in Sainte-Marie-de-Kent**, is a cozy and secluded log cabin restaurant nestled in a maple forest paradise. The licensed restaurant serves up traditional meals when the sap is running and offers a splendid place to enjoy an early spring afternoon. A truly unique experience.

5. **The Maison de la fondue in Tracadie-Sheila** is another one of those New Brunswick hidden gems. Since 1992, this establishment has served various fondues, as well as seafood and other prepared dishes. This is one place that absolutely has to be on everyone's to-do list.

TOP FIVE EVENTS IN NEW BRUNSWICK'S LABOUR HISTORY

David Frank teaches Canadian history at the University of New Brunswick in Fredericton. He has published J.B. McLachlan: A Biography *and is a former editor of the regional history journal* Acadiensis. *He is currently directing a project of research and activity called "Re-Connecting with the History of Labour in New Brunswick", which can be visited at www.lhtnb.ca.*

1. When it was organized by Saint John longshoremen in 1849, they simply called it the Laborers' Benevolent Association. It became one of the strongest unions in Saint John and reminds us that New Brunswick was one of the early birthplaces of unionism in Canada. This pioneer union later helped establish the New Brunswick Federation of Labour (1913), one of the oldest in Canada, and continues today as a local of the International Longshoremen's Association.

2. Labour is a form of human capital, and nobody explained the underlying need for workers to protect their investment better than John Davidson, Professor of Political Economy and Moral and Mental Philosophy at the University of New Brunswick, in his 1898 book, The Bargain Theory of Wages: "It is labor that is bought and sold but, with the labor, goes the laborer. Therefore instead of a great simplification we have a great complication."

3. Modern labour laws came out of the experiences of the Great Depression in the 1930s. When workers in Minto and on the Miramichi went out on strike against mine operators and mill owners in 1937 and 1938, they did not achieve all their goals, but they did win a Labour and Industrial Relations Act, one of the first laws in Canada to protect the right to union membership and collective bargaining.

4. Public sector workers in New Brunswick won the right to collective bargaining in 1968, when Liberal Louis Robichaud was premier, but in 1992 they had to go on strike to defend that right when Liberal Frank McKenna was premier. Under an Expenditure Management Act, the government was claiming it could disregard contracts with its own employees. Public sector unions led a short, successful strike to force the government to live up to its agreements.

5. Unions are part of the democratic way of life in New Brunswick, and membership levels (about 30 per cent of the work force) are about the

ame as in other provinces. They are often busy defending past achievements, but the changing economy is always presenting new organizing challenges in the workplace. Meanwhile, unions also work to advance the interests of all workers, unionized or not, in areas such as employment standards, pay equity, education, health and safety which can help protect the social and human capital of the province.

TOP FIVE POETS IN NEW BRUNSWICK HISTORY

Donna Allard — aka Acadian Rose — is an Anglophone born poet living in New Brunswick. She is currently President of the Canadian Poetry Association, editor of the CPA magazine POEMATA, and founder of Chocolate River Poetry Association & festival (Chocolate River Poets & Chocolate River Readings). For several years she served on the board of directors for the National Milton Acorn Festival PEI.
Her first book of poetry titled: Minago Streets will be launched at the Chocolate River Festival this year.

1- **The Honourable Rita Joe,**" poet laureate" of the Mi'kmaq Nation, started writing in her 30s to challenge the negative images of Aboriginal people being taught to her children. Her books include The Poems of Rita Joe, Songs of Eskasoni: More Poems of Rita Joe, Lnu and Indians We're Called, and Songs of Rita Joe: The Autobiography of a Mi'kmaq Poet.

2- **Acadian Poet Gerald Leblanc:** A prolific poet and "ambassador of Acadian poetry," Leblanc was also a founder of Éditions Perce-Neige, a Moncton-based publishing company.

3- **Our Herménégilde Chiasson Lieutenant-Governor of New Brunswick** is one of Canada's most accomplished cultural icons. Winner of the Governor General Award for poetry; Award winning film director and artist, he is also an honourary member of the Canadian Poetry Association.

4. Born in Douglas, New Brunswick, in 1860, **Charles G.D. Roberts** was known as the father of Canadian Poetry. He was a poet and prose writer who inspired creativity in other poets of his generation, among them Bliss Carman (his cousin), Archibald Lampman and Duncan Campbell Scott. Together, these four poets became known as the "Confederation" poets.

5- **Dr. Fred Cogswell** made an outstanding contribution to New Brunswick as a professor, scholar, editor, publisher, translator and writer, as well as an important friend of poets and writers. He was the founder of Fiddlehead Poetry Books and editor of Fiddlehead magazine. A unique contribution is Fred Cogswell's translation of French speaking poets in Canada.

TAKE 5: BRAD WOODSIDE'S FIVE
MOST INFLUENTIAL NEW BRUNSWICKERS

Brad Woodside is one of the most recognizable and longest-serving politicians currently holding office in New Brunswick. This mayor of Fredericton was first elected to Fredericton city council in May 1981 and became mayor five years later. Woodside held this position until 1999 and made a return in 2004. Always passionate about the city he calls home, Woodside dedicates his time to a number of organization and causes. The former talk-show host and announcer for CFNB Radio is a dynamic speaker, and one not afraid to speak his mind. Woodside shares with us his votes for the five most inspirational New Brunswickers, all of whom have made contributions to their communities and province.

1. **Louis Robichaud:** For implementing equal opportunity health care and education for all New Bruswickers.

2. **The Irving family:** In good and bad, they have provided many employment opportunities for New Brunswickers.

TAKE FIVE

3. The McCain family: They created a international frozen food empire headquartered in Florenceville and have thus provided many opportunities for employment.

4. David Ganong: Creator of a St. Stephen candy empire, his products are shipped to customers all over the world.

5. Frank McKenna: He was inspirational, motivational and worked hard convincing New Brunswickers they were not have-nots. They were can-dos.

TAKE 5: BERNARD RIORDON'S TOP FIVE WORDS THAT BEST DESCRIBE NEW BRUNSWICK

There are few people in New Brunswick as respected as Bernard Riordon. Born in Bathurst, Riordon is director and CEO of the Beaverbrook Art Gallery in Fredericton. Previously, Mr. Riordon served as Director and CEO of the Art Gallery of Nova Scotia for 30 years, during which time he built that institution from its humble origins to a widely respected and dynamic institution. In addition to his arts administration expertise, Riordan is a curator and writer. Riordon gives us five words he thinks describes New Brunswick. He explains, "From my perspective, New Brunswick is a province whose greatest strength is its people. We are honest, hardworking and resourceful. The physical beauty of the province is evident throughout and it is truly the 'picture province'. Cultural diversity and artistic excellence characterize the province and make it a creative and stimulating place to work and live."

1) **Picturesque**

2) **Industrious**

3) **Peaceful**

4) **Stimulating**

5) **Culturally Diverse**

TAKE 5: POUL JORGENSEN'S AND BRIAN CLARK'S TOP FIVE HIKING TRAILS

Poul Jorgensen is the executive director of the New Brunswick Trails Council Inc. and Brian Clarke has managed the Fundy Trial since it opened in September 1998; he's also worked in the hotel industry and is currently co-chair of the Bay of Fundy Tourism Partnership, president of Hospitality Saint John, chair of the Saint John Fundy Heritage Zone, and Treasurer of the New Brunswick Trails Council Inc.

1.**Tracadie-Sheila to Clifton and Shippagan:** From Tracadie-Sheila to Inkerman and then on to Pokeshaw, the Sentier New Brunswick Trail System Route # 5 runs through the heart of New Brunswick's Acadian Peninsula. Built on an abandoned rail line, this trail showcases spectacular seaside views, the smell of salt air, and an insight into the lively Acadian culture.

2. **Woodstock to Muniac:** Follow Sentier New Brunswick Trail System from Woodstock to Muniac. The Sentier New Brunswick Trail system provides a great way to explore a rural New Brunswick community along the majestic Saint John River. This multi-use trail, built on abandoned Canadian Pacific rail line, is perfect for any type of trail user. Its gentle grades and multiple access points allow you to tailor an adventure to suit your personal needs — from a short walk to a multi-day trek on foot or bicycle. Time to complete this section of trail on foot is approximately one day. Cycling this trail is a leisurely four-hour trip.

3. Muniac to Grand Falls: Ambling from Muniac to Grand Falls, the Sentier New Brunswick Trail provides visitors with a glimpse of rural New Brunswick, past and present. This multi-use trail, built on old Canadian Pacific rail line, is perfect for any type of use. Gentle grades and easy access points let you tailor your own adventure.

4. Fundy Trail's Fundy Footpath: "A 32-mile stretch of coastline with no towns or roads. This is how National Geographic Adventure Magazine described it. "Here, the deserted shoreline alternates between wave-pounded cliffs and rocky beaches backed by wooded ravines where deer, moose, bobcats, and the occasional bear prowl."

5. Fundy Trail: Until the first phase of the Fundy Trail Parkway opened six summers ago along the Bay off Fundy, this stretch of New Brunswick coastline was one of the longest pieces of undeveloped oceanfront between Labrador and Florida.

TAKE 5: BERNARD IMBEAULT'S TOP FIVE
NEW BRUNSWICKER'S HE ADMIRES MOST

Bernard Imbeault, president and co-founder of Moncton-based Pizza Delight Corporation, took an idea in the late 1960s and turned it into a popular national pizza restaurant chain. Starting in Shediac with a small take-out restaurant named Pizza Delight, the company used its unique recipes to create what became a national hit. More than 110 Pizza Delight restaurants now welcome customers across Canada and Imbeault is considered by many as a New Brunswick business genius. He shares with us the five New Brunswickers he most admires.

1. K.C. Irving: He had a long-range vision and pushed it to the limit. He made a good intergenerational transfer of the family business.

2. **Harrison McCain:** A dynamic entrepreneur, he put Atlantic Canadian business on the world map.

3. **Lord Beaverbrook:** He gave philanthropy a boost in New Brunswick and was an entrepreneur extraordinaire.

4. **Father Clément Cormier:** He built an institution that changed the Acadian psyche (the Université de Moncton). A great promoter of excellence and a quiet leader, his influence extended throughout New Brunswick Society.

5. **Antonine Maillet:** She put New Brunswickers and Acadians on the international scene. She is a genial writer able to use the simple word or a truly poetic sentence without ever forgetting humour.